Animals and Birds

Coloring Book

for Kids

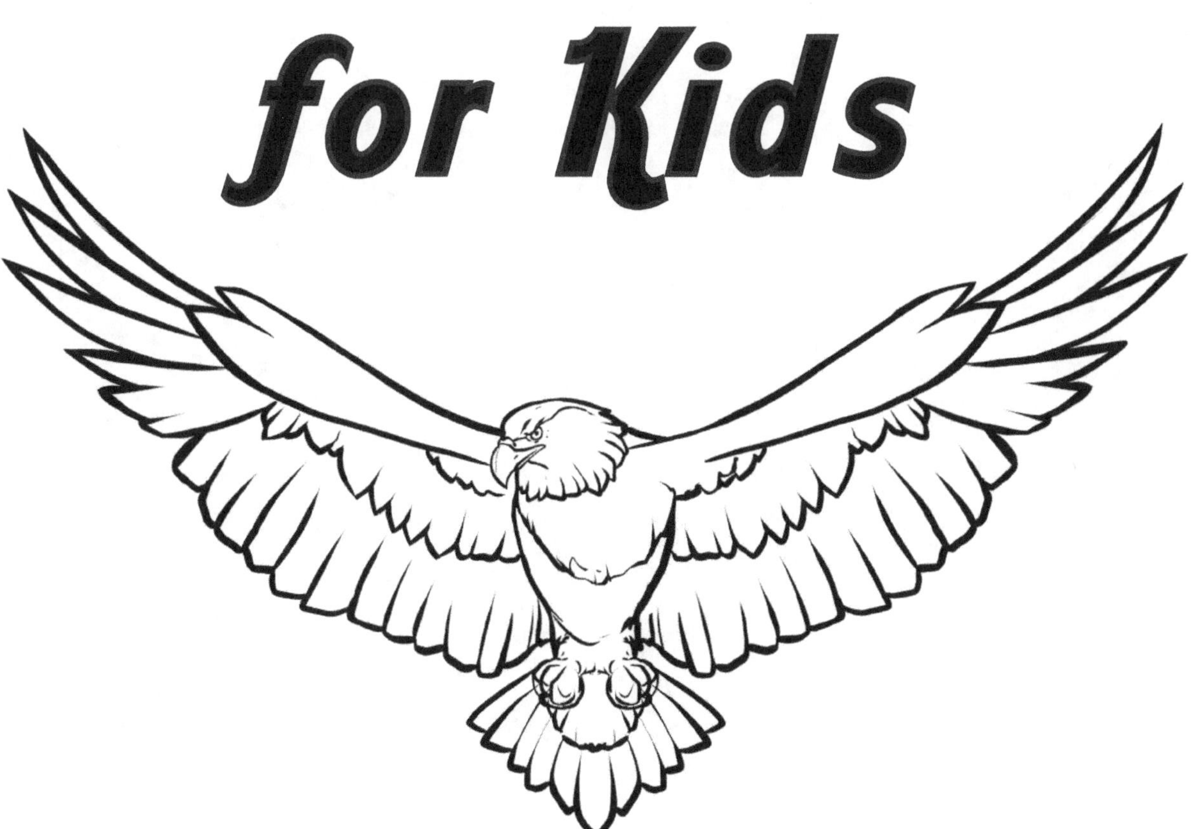

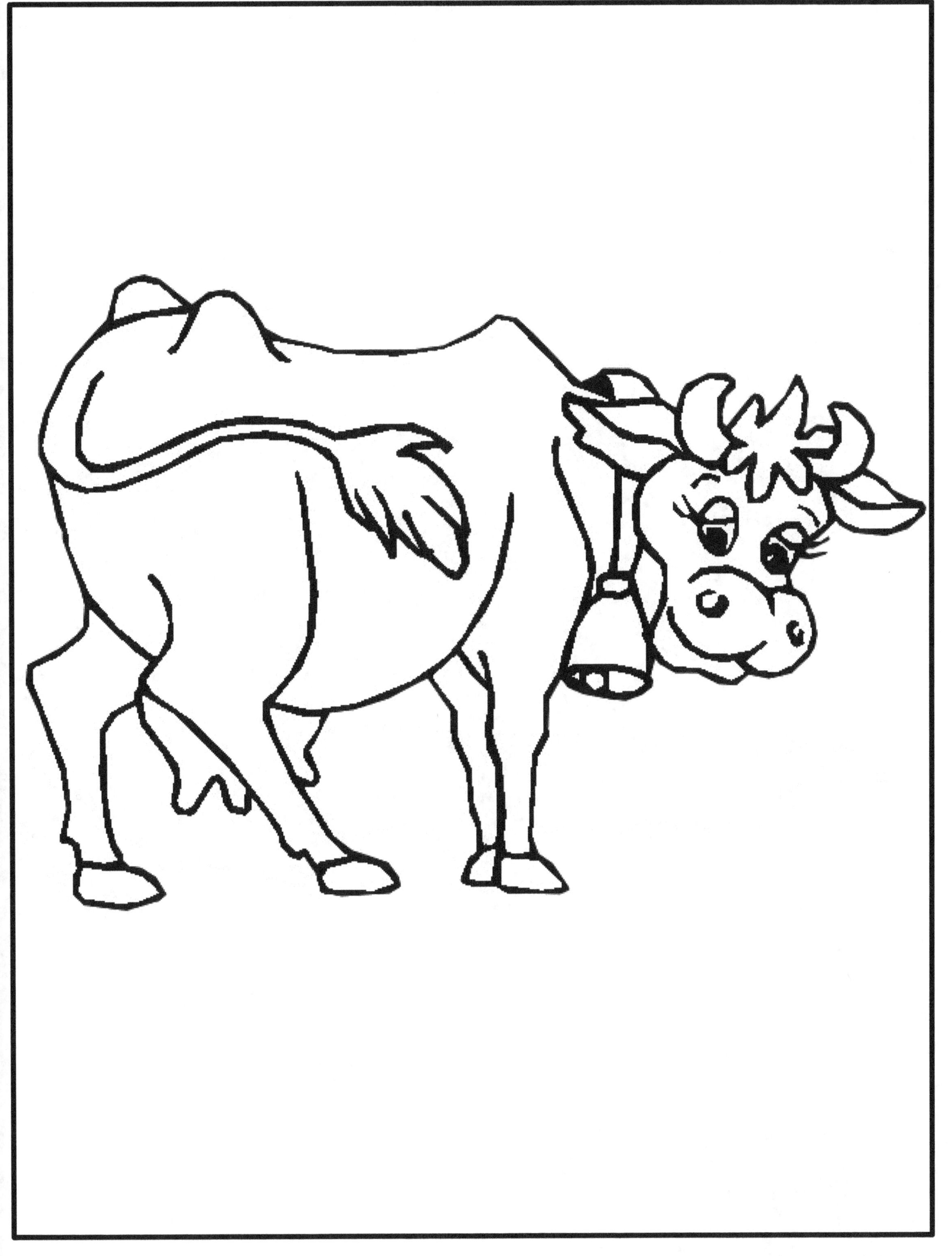

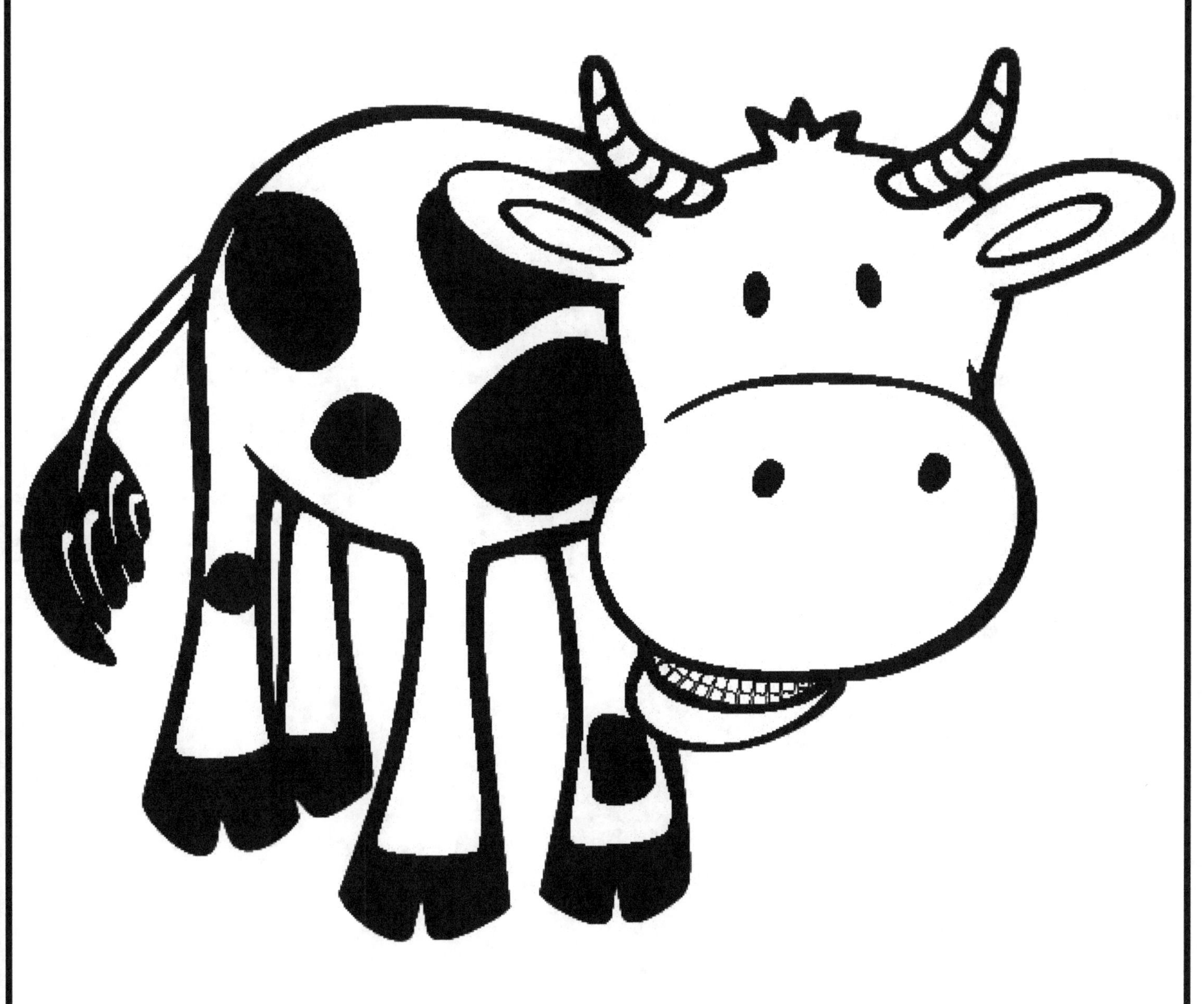

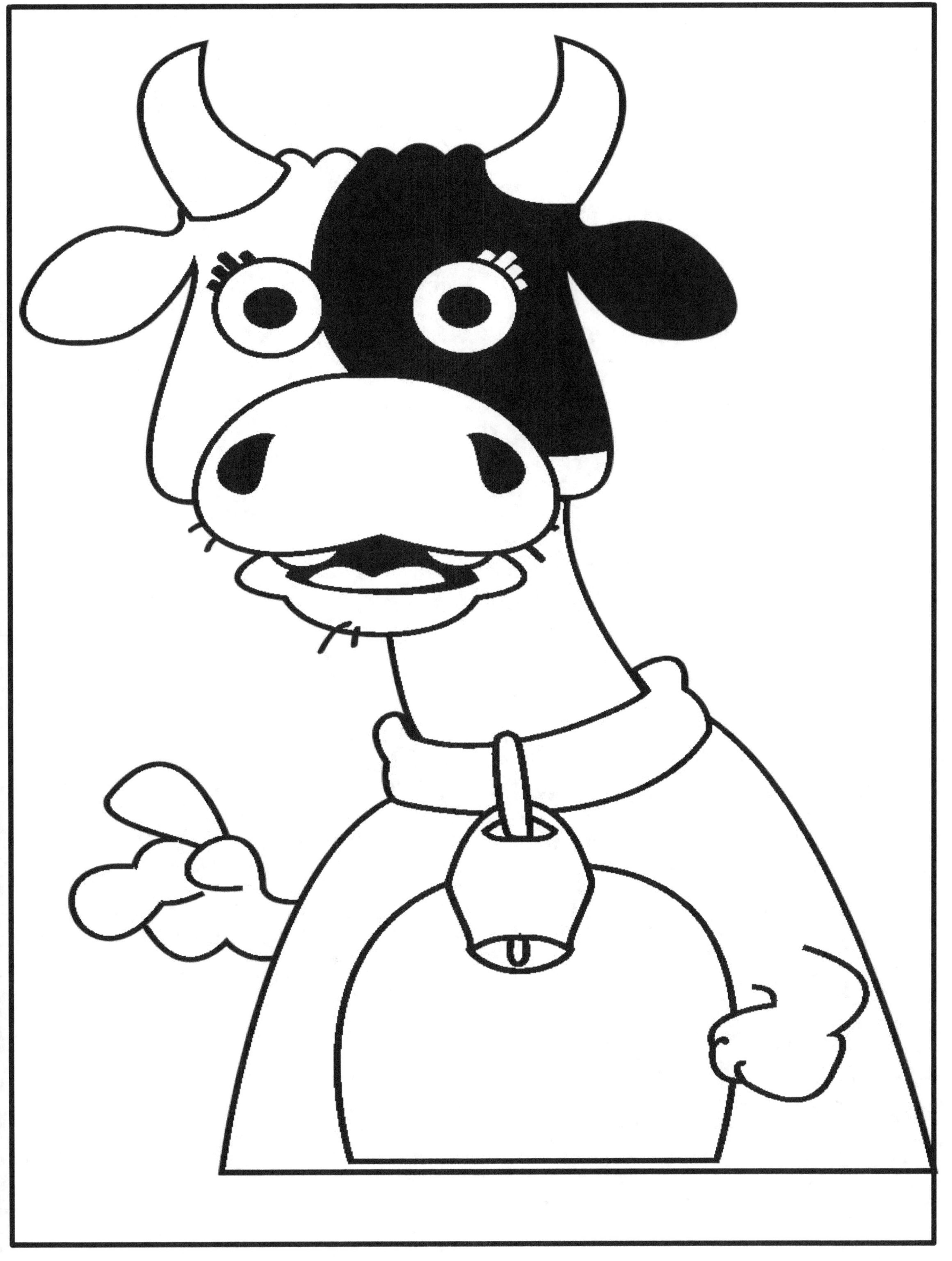

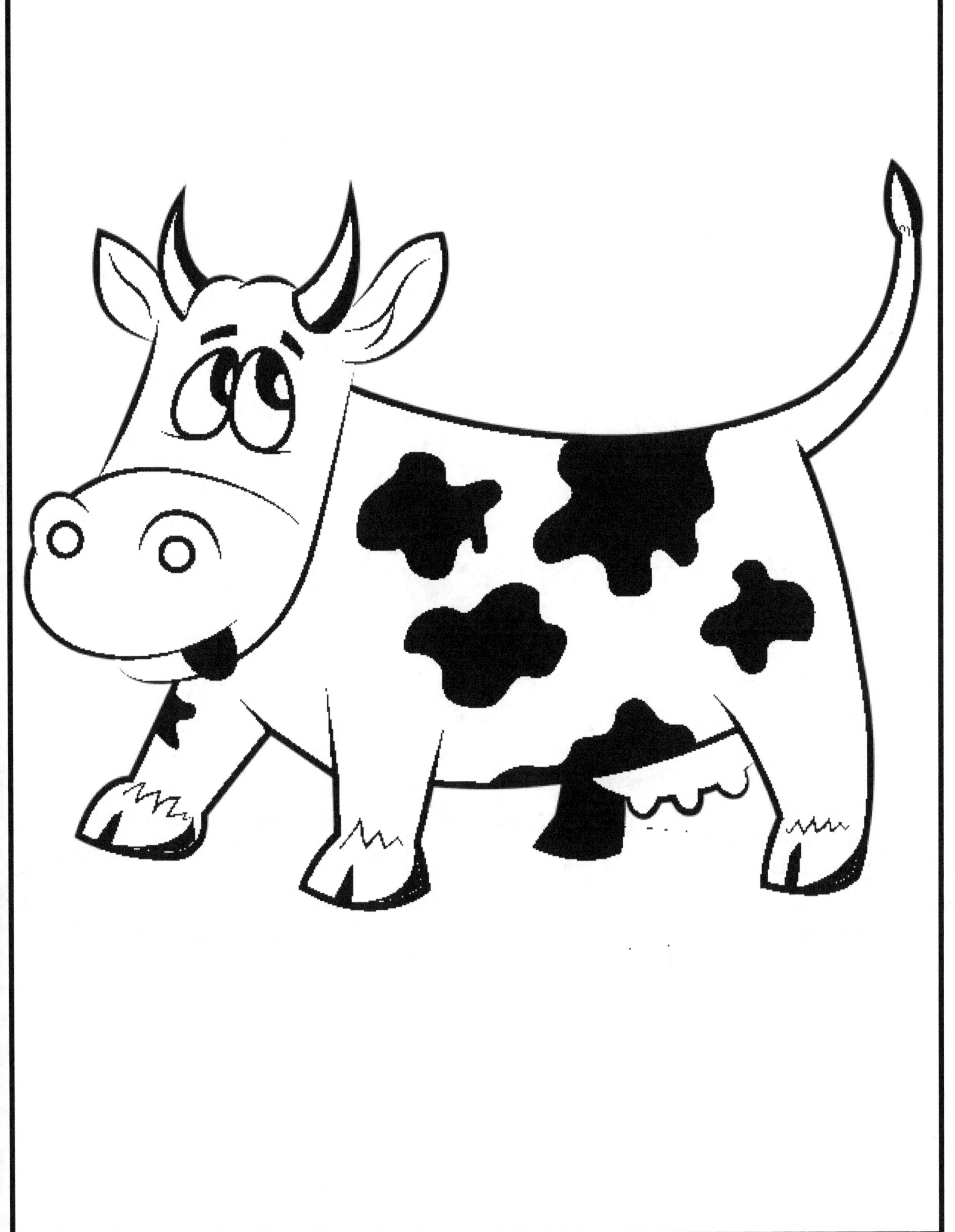

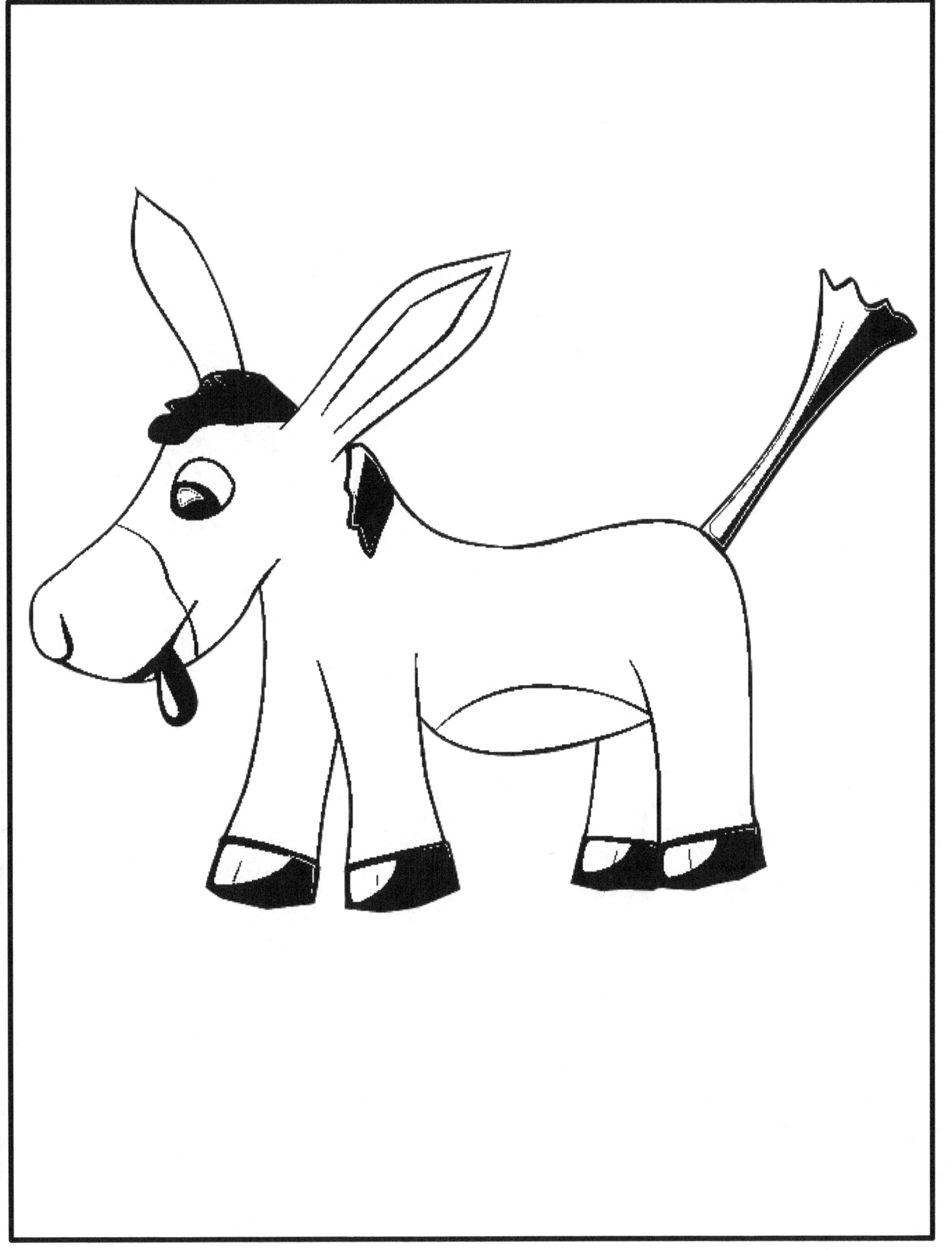

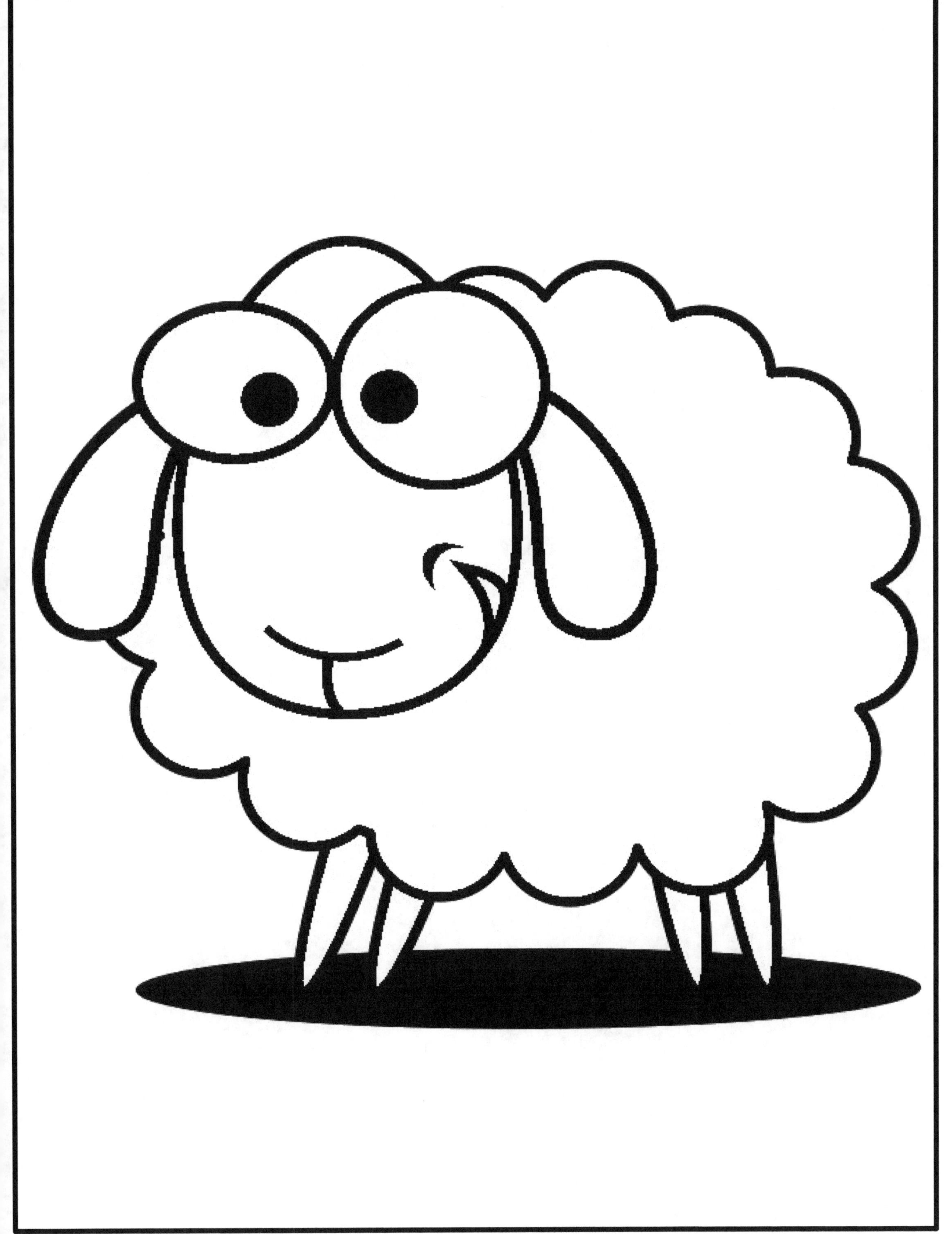

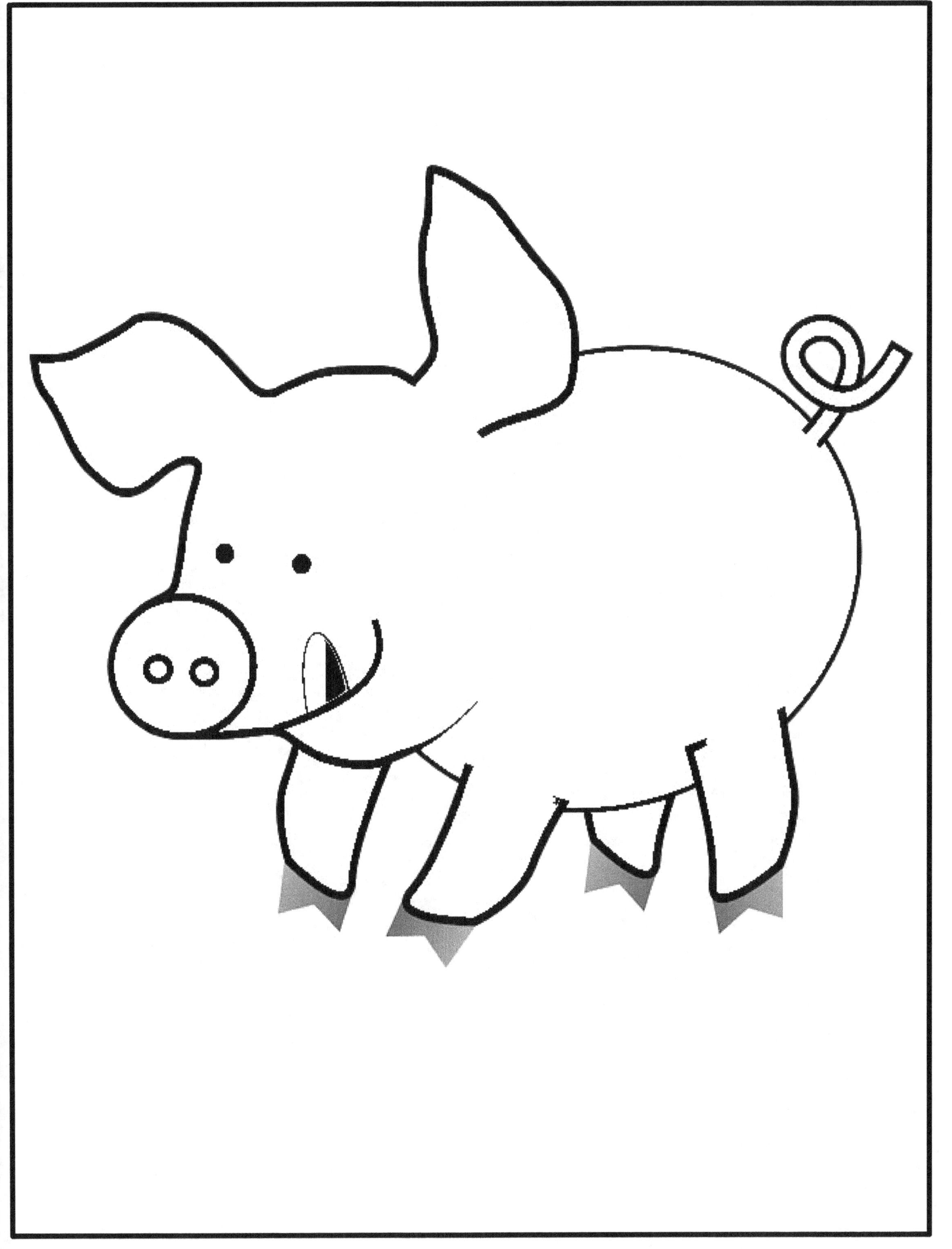

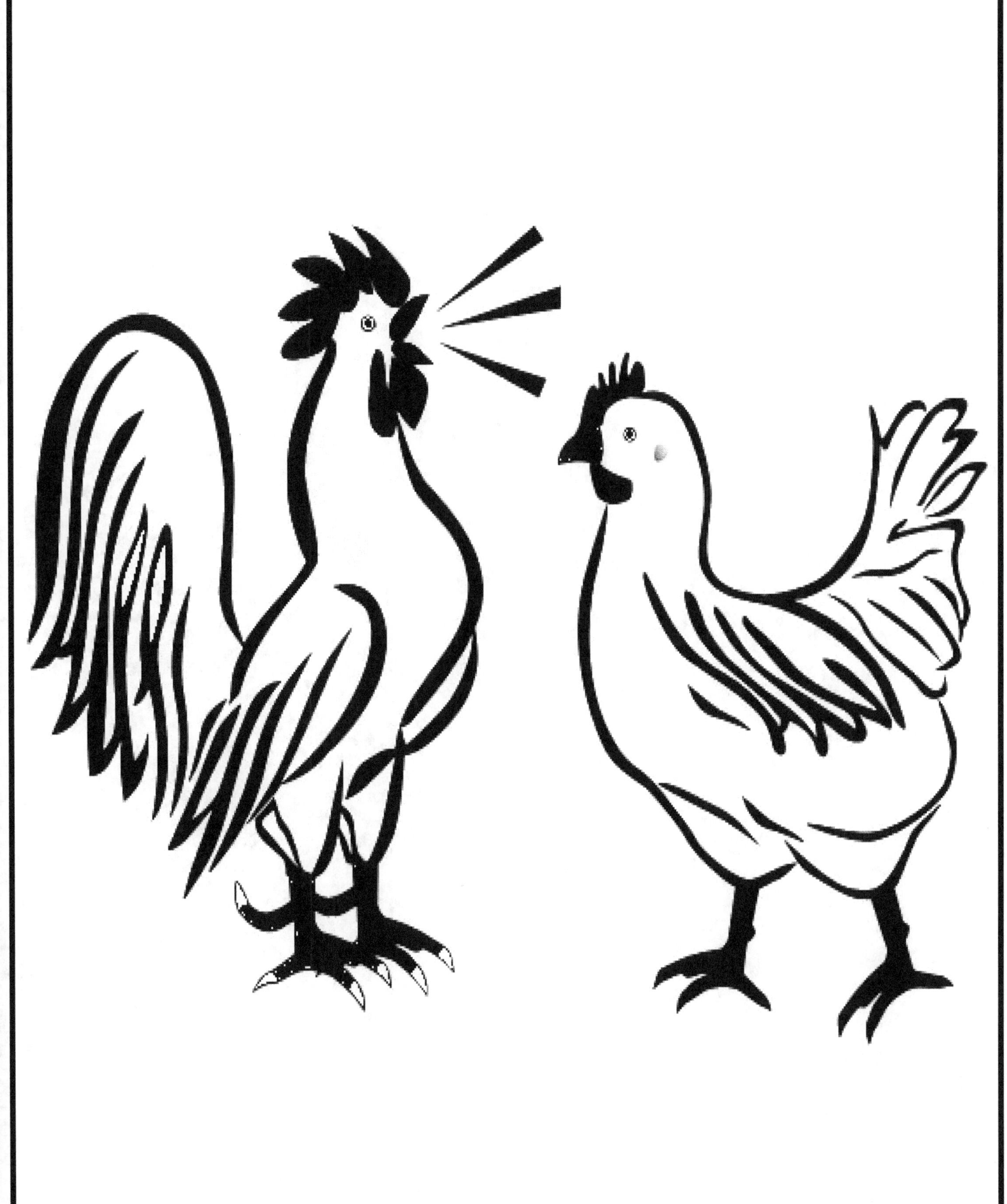

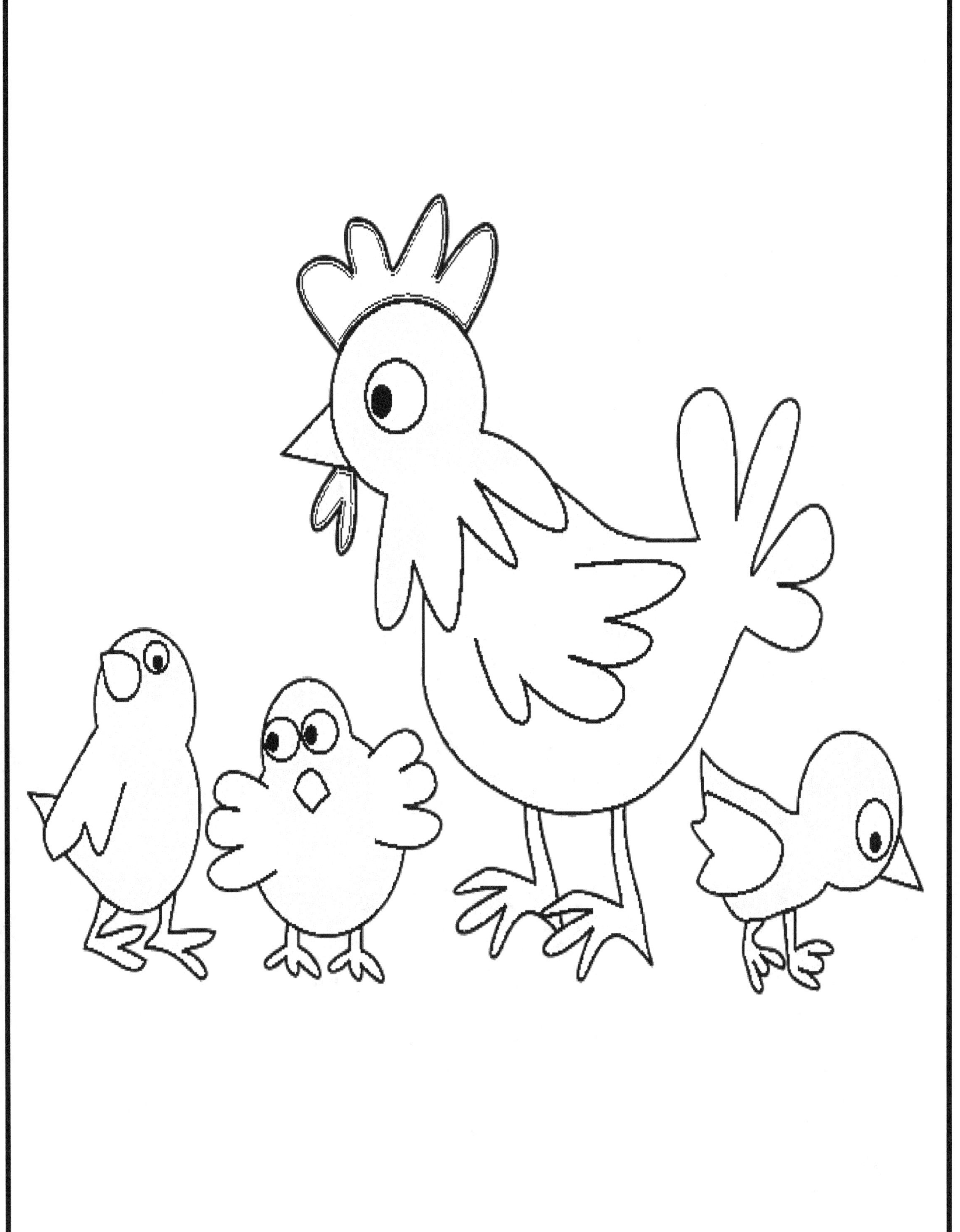

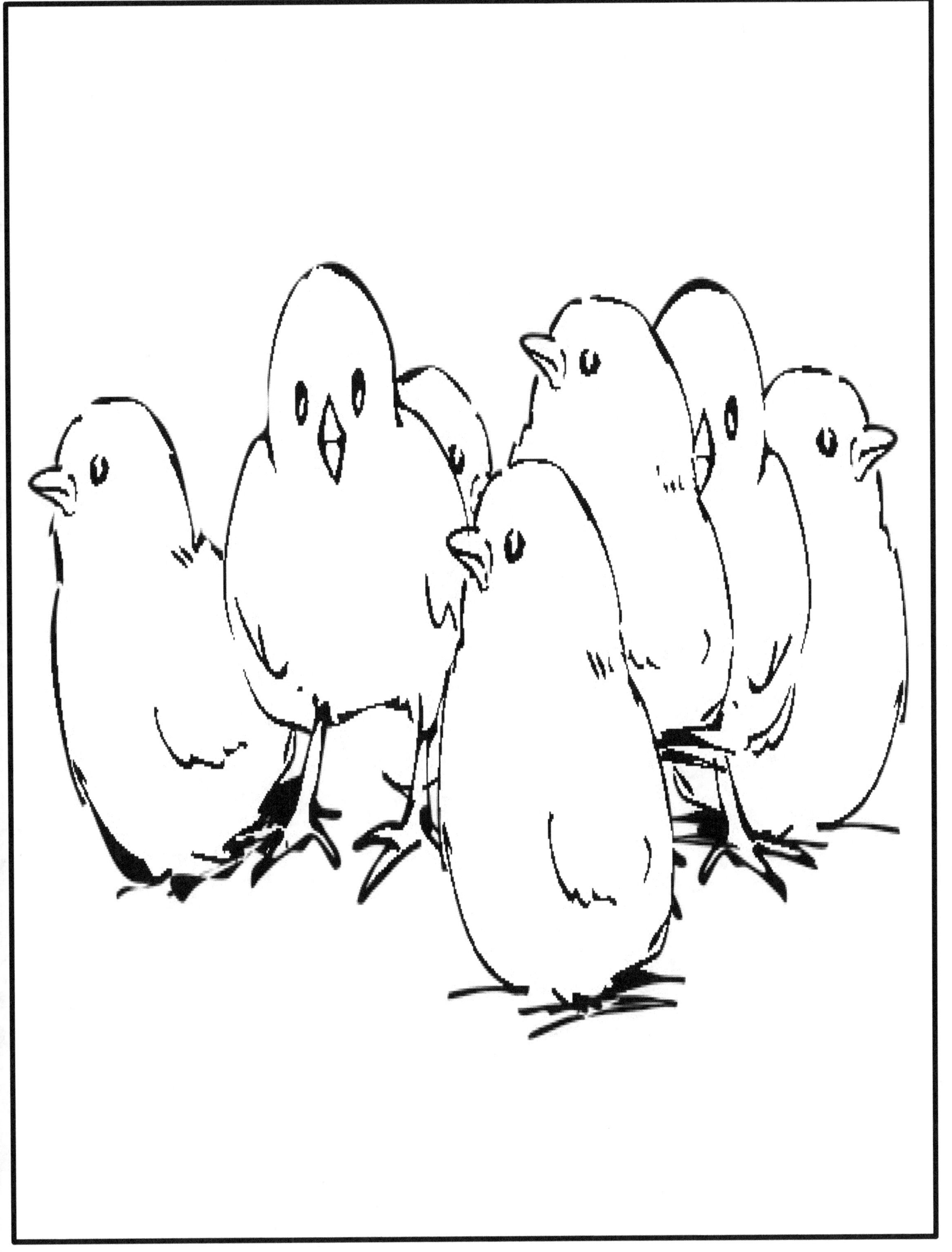

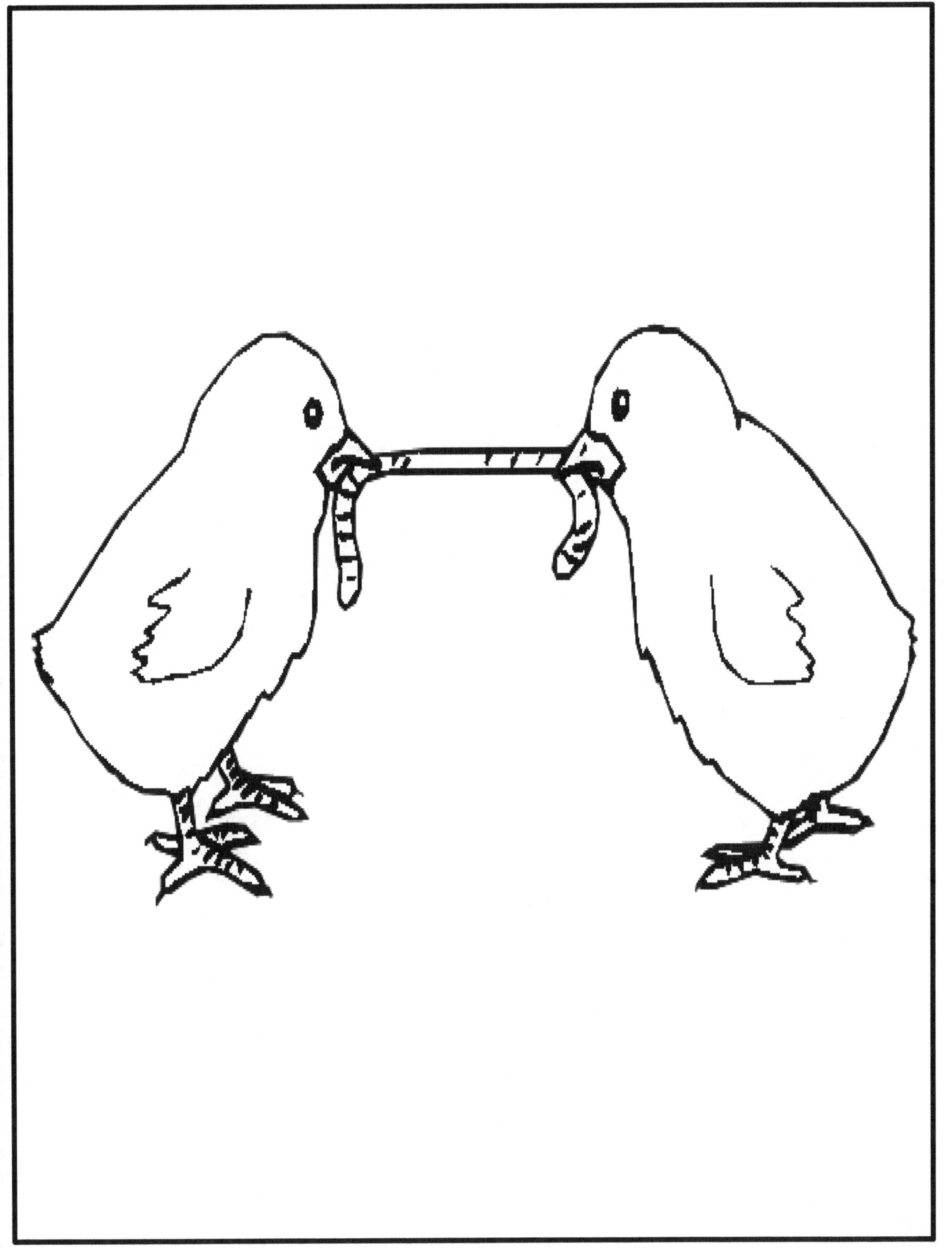

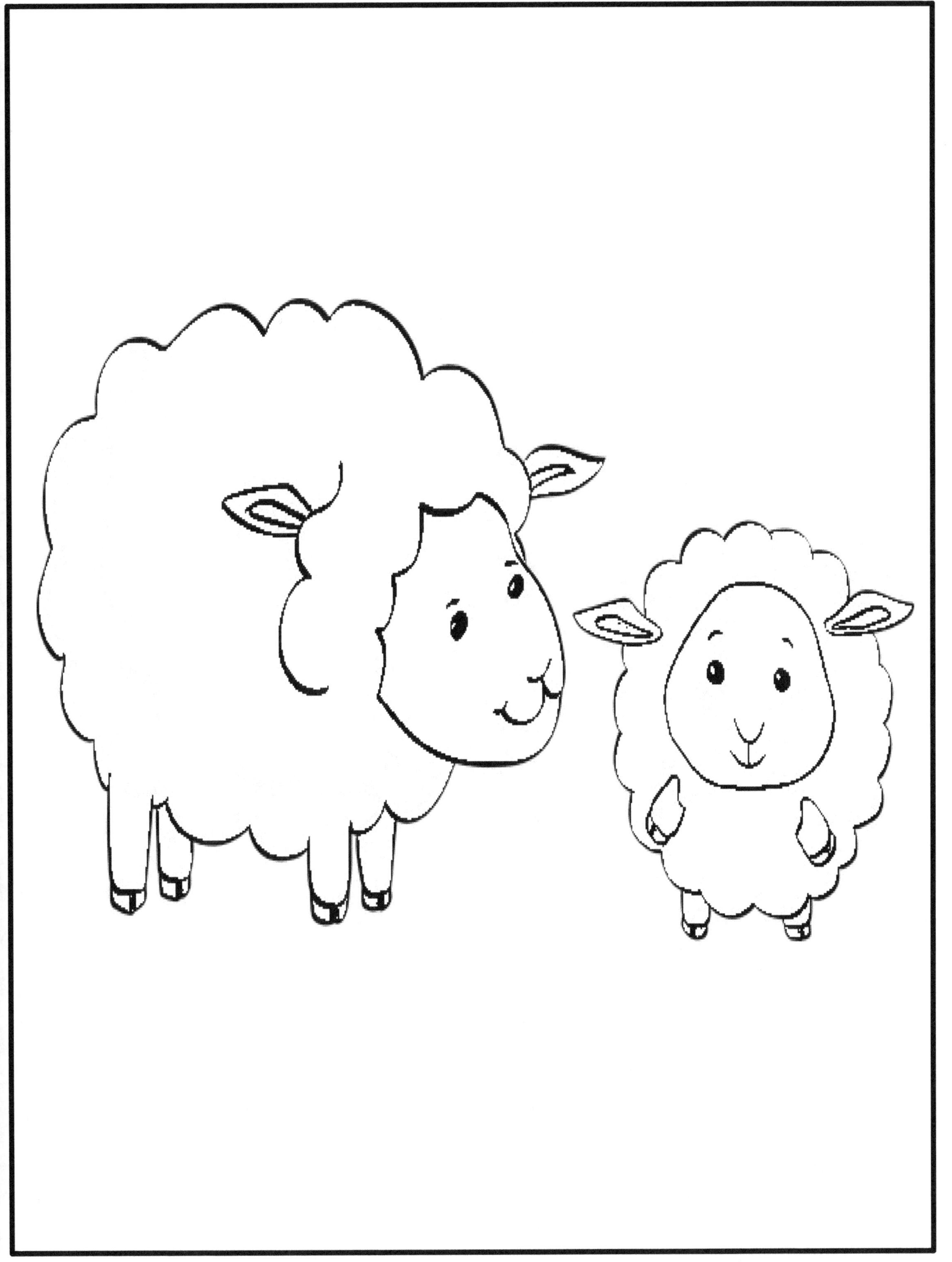

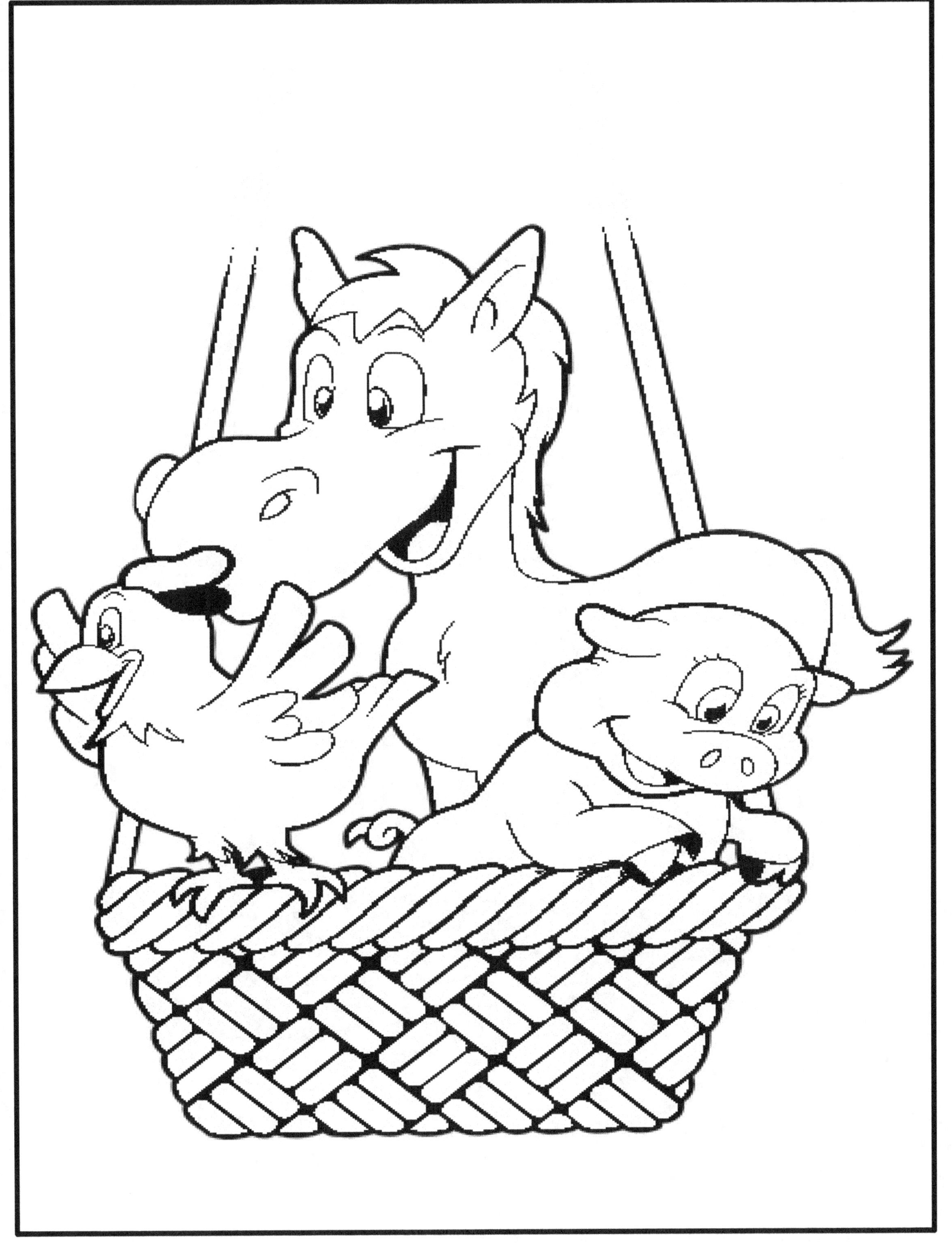

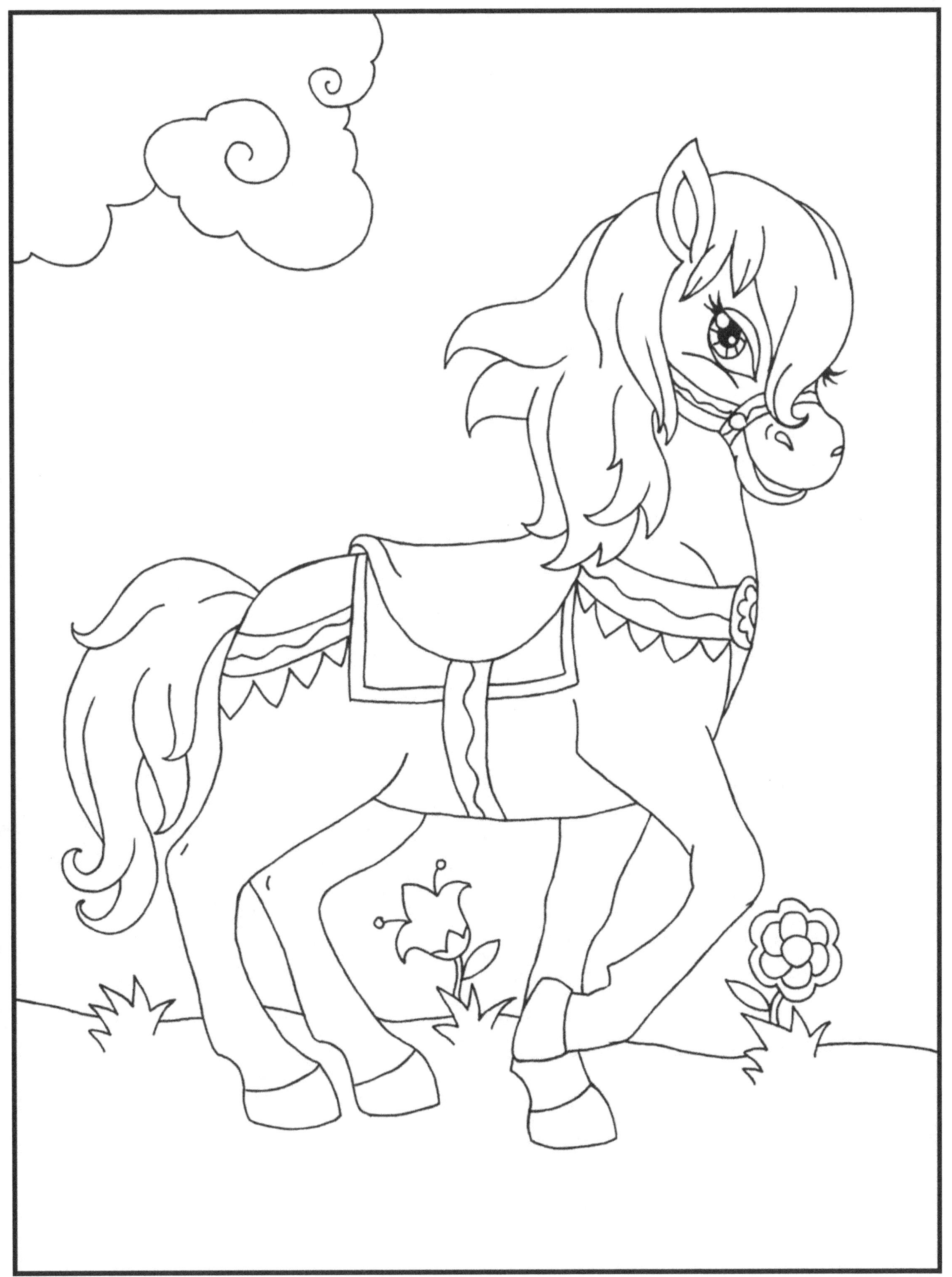

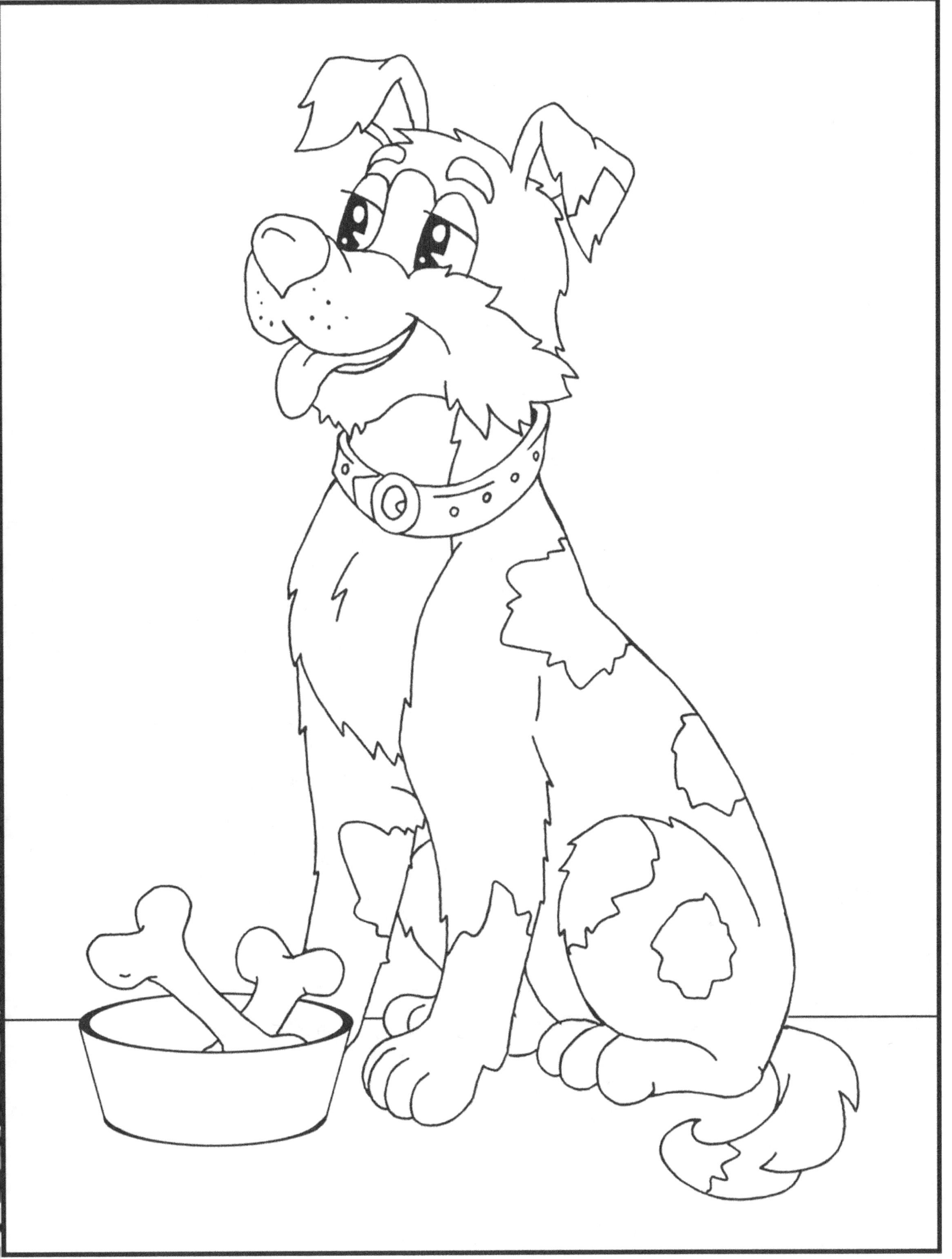

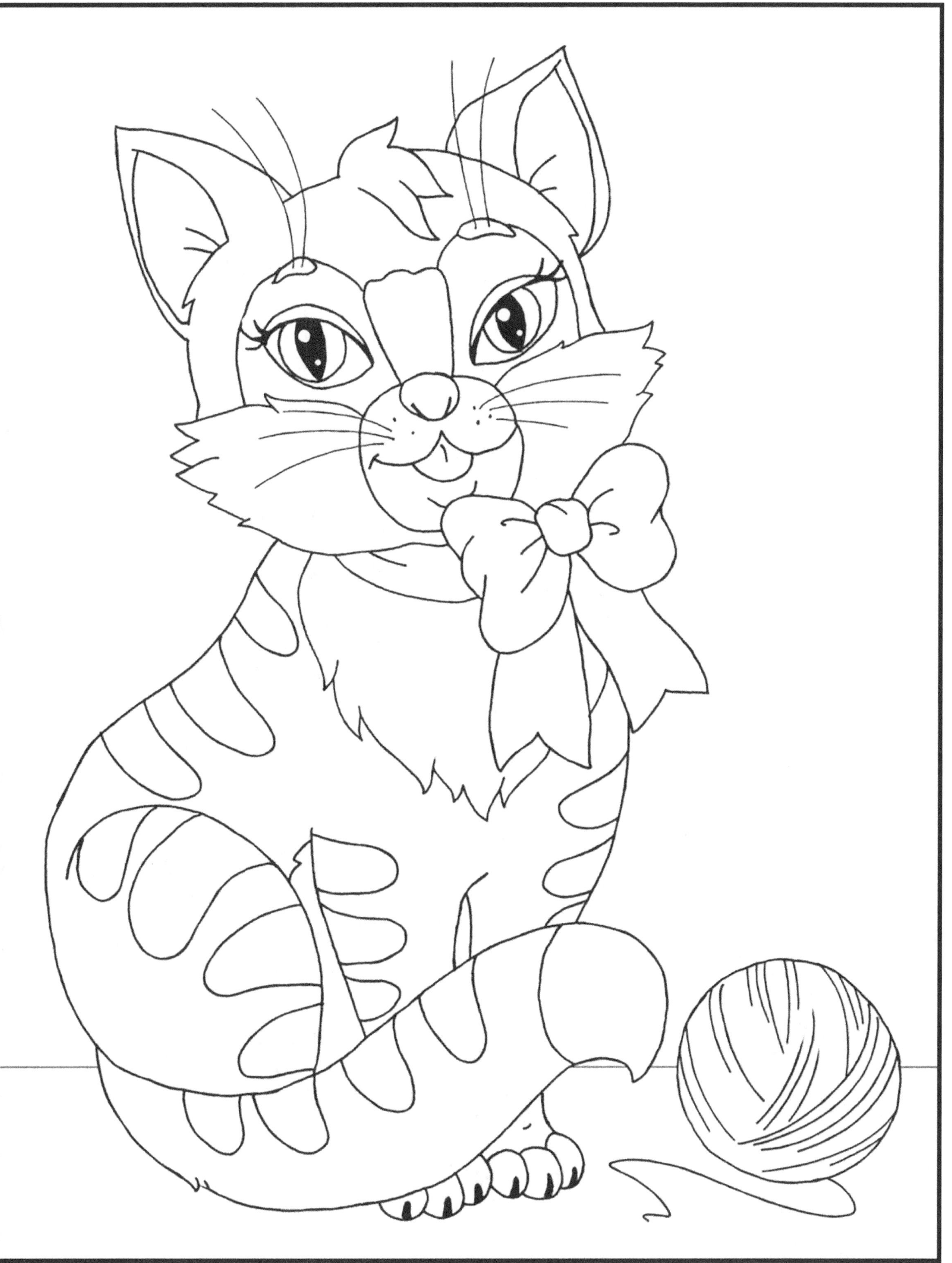

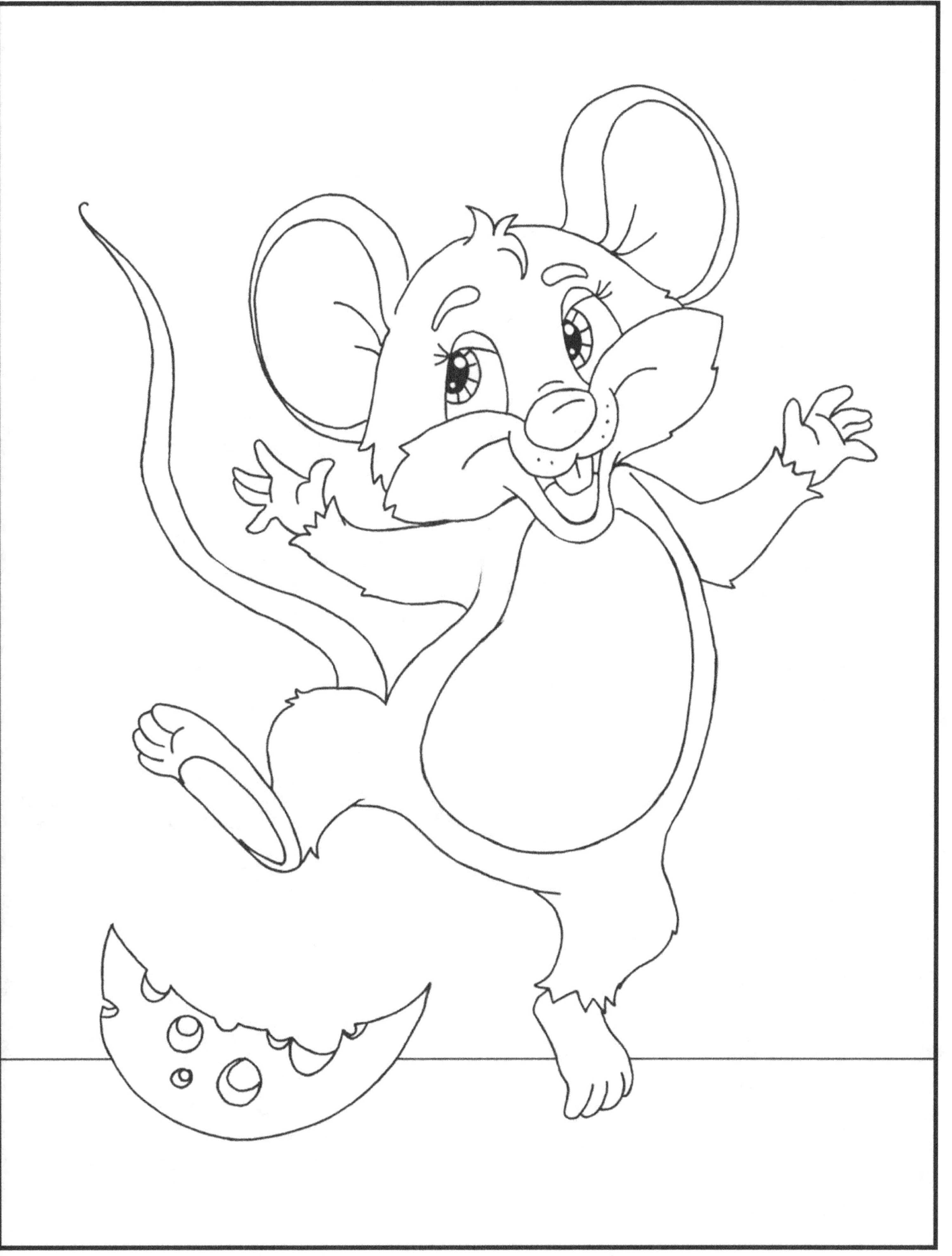

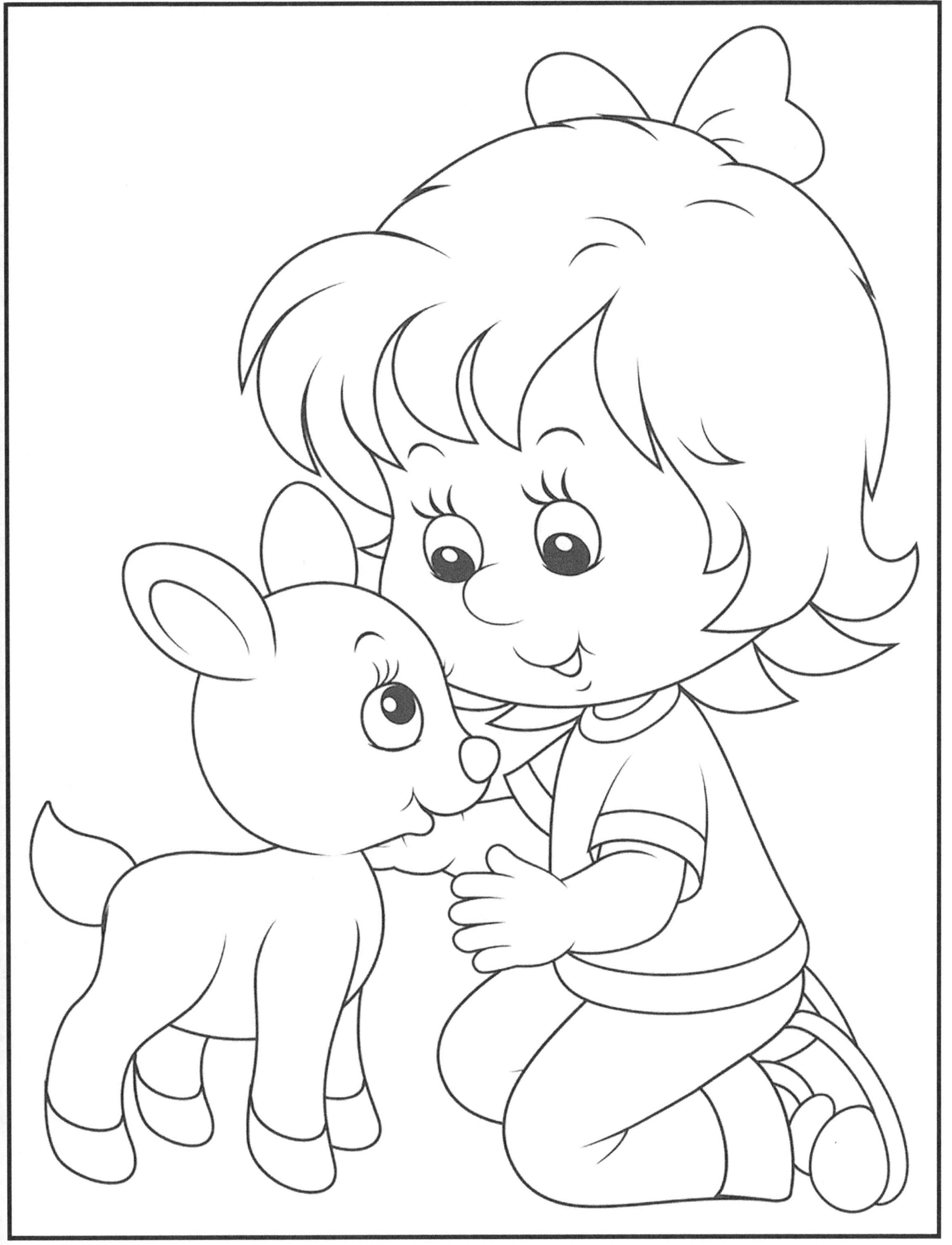

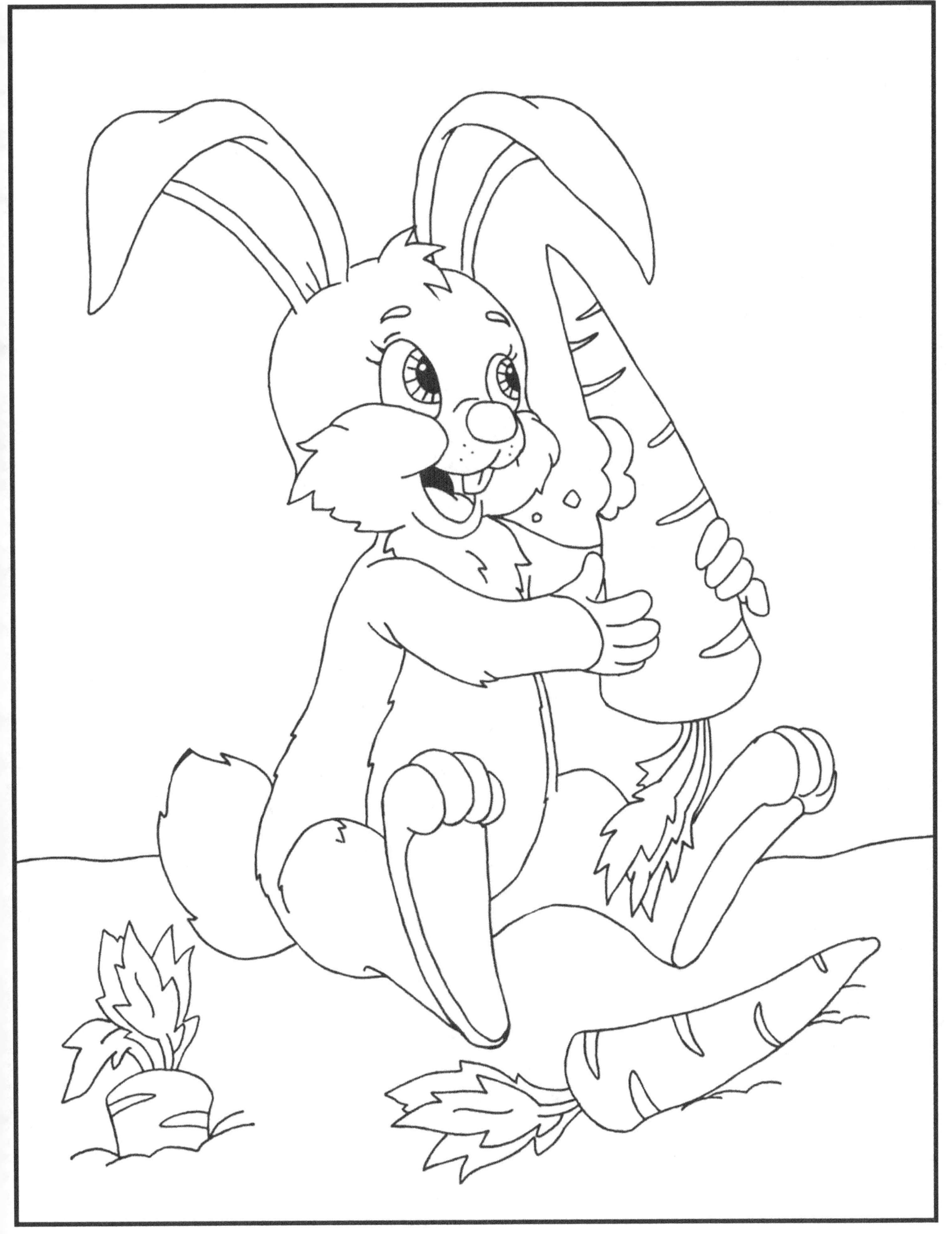

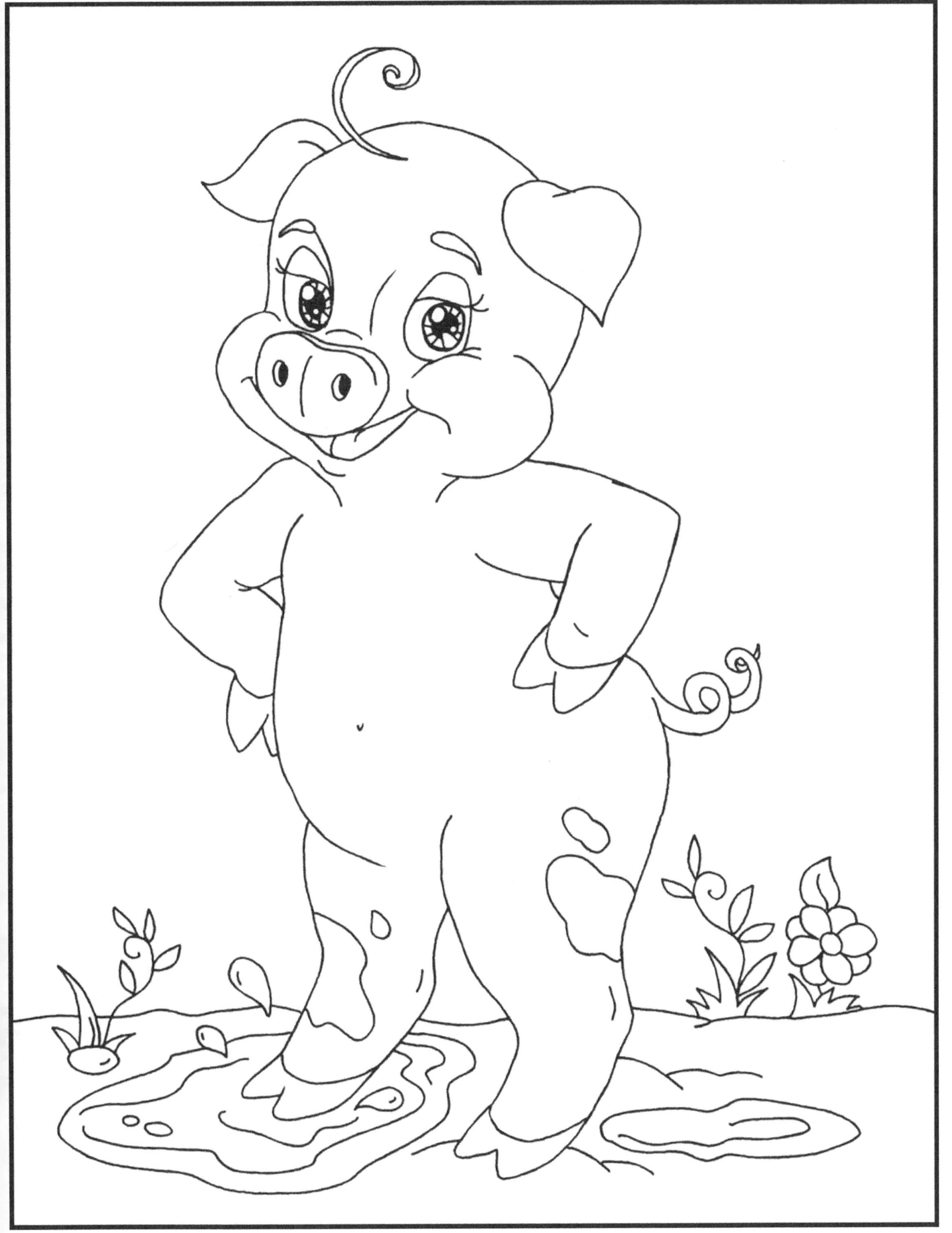

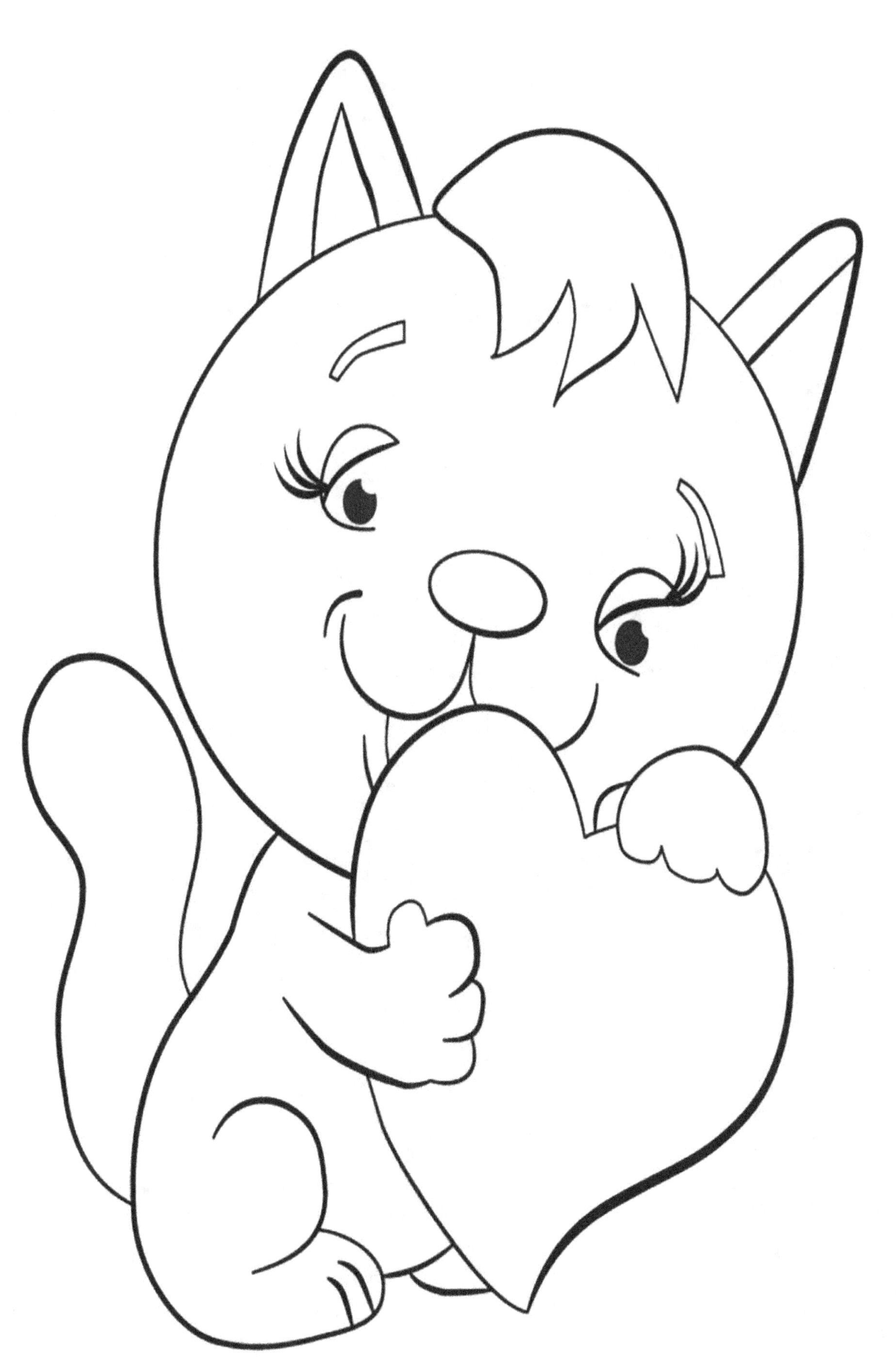

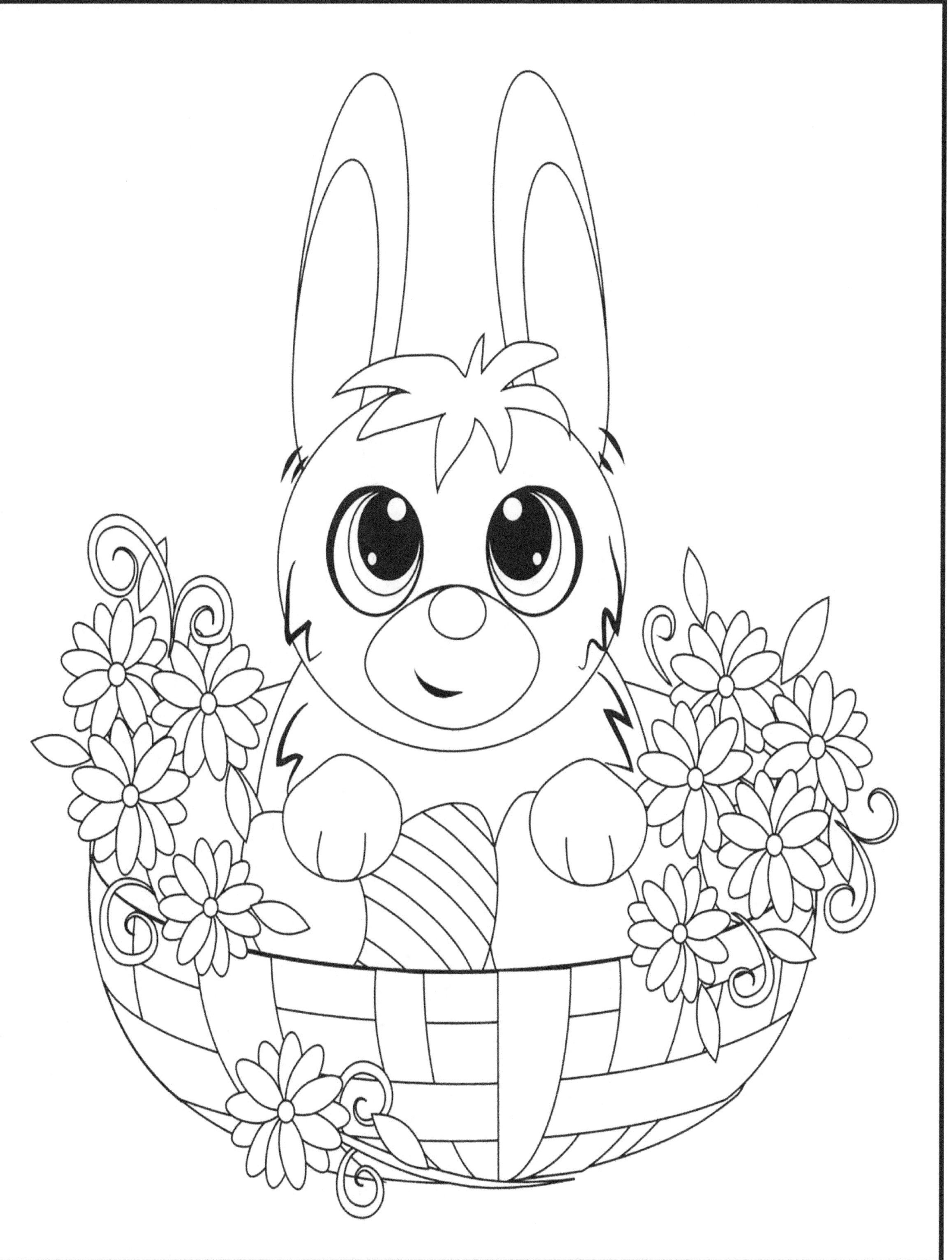

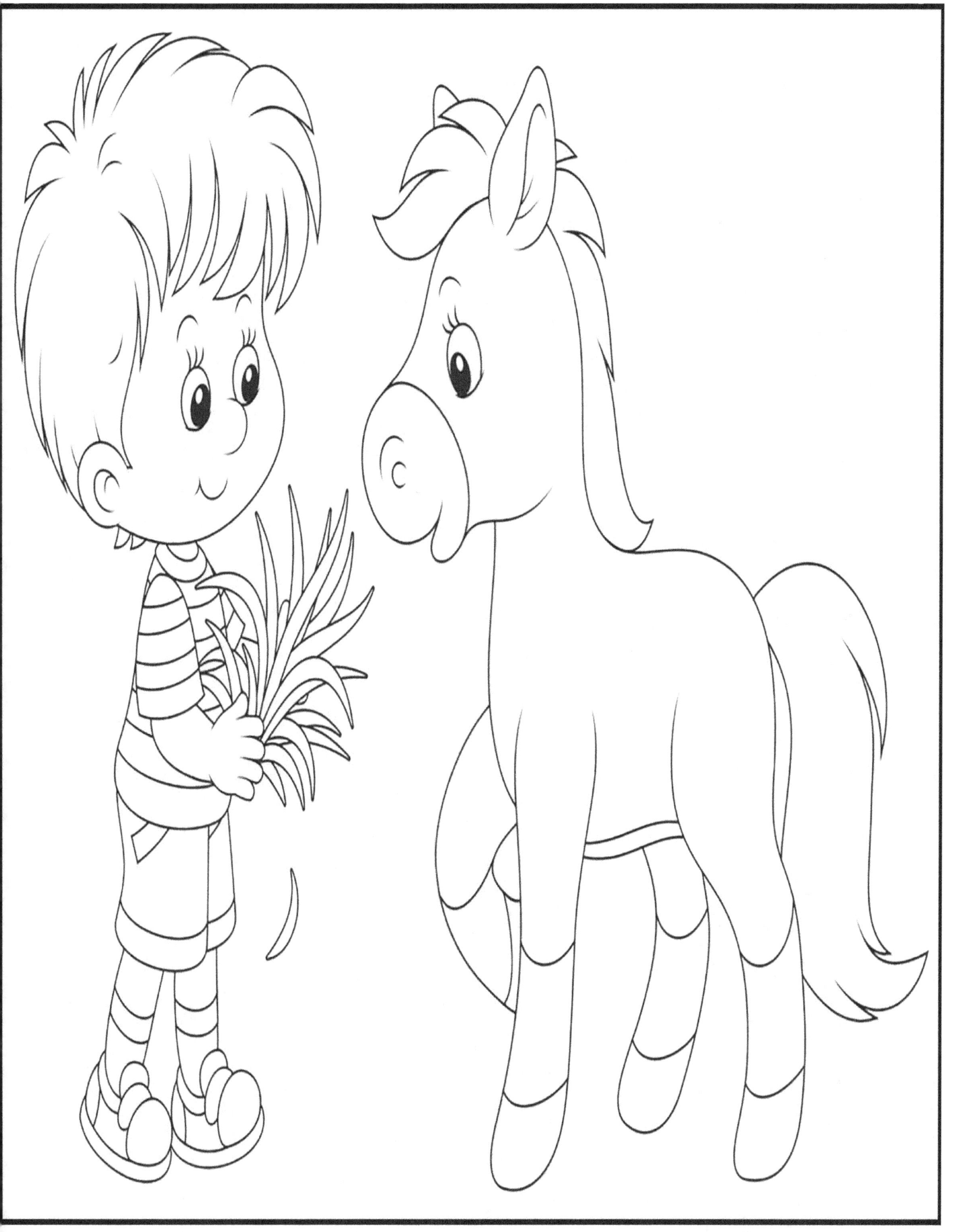

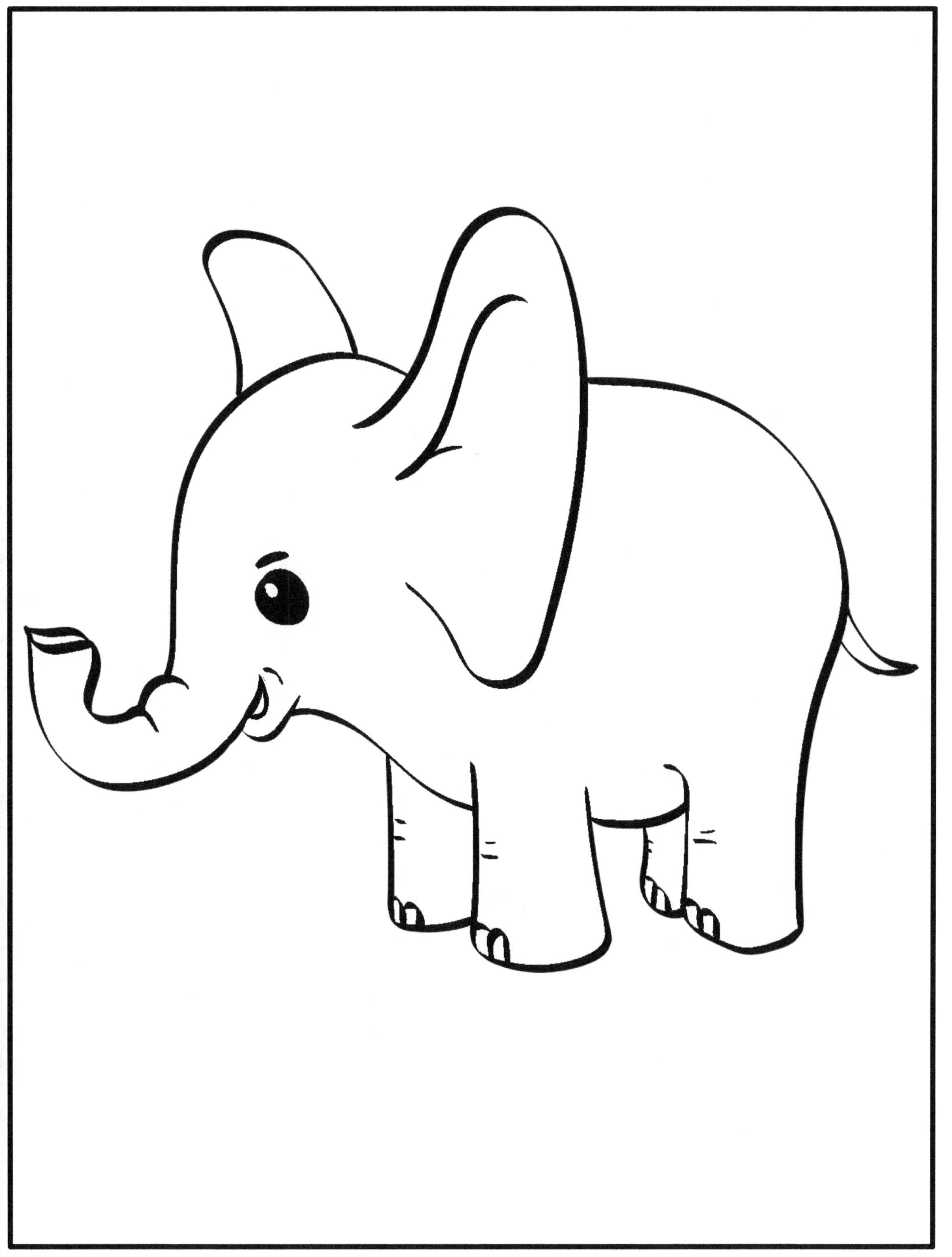

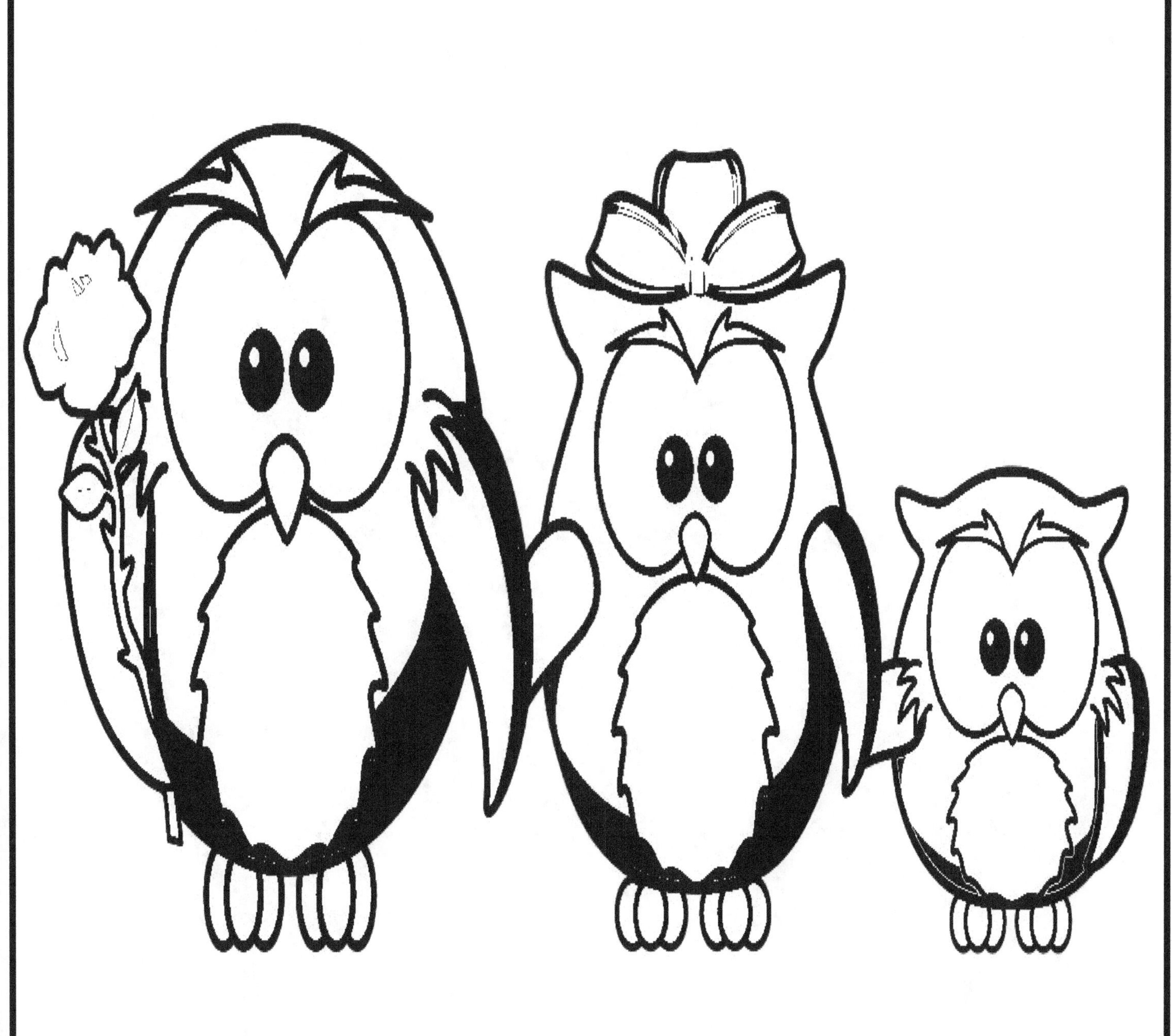

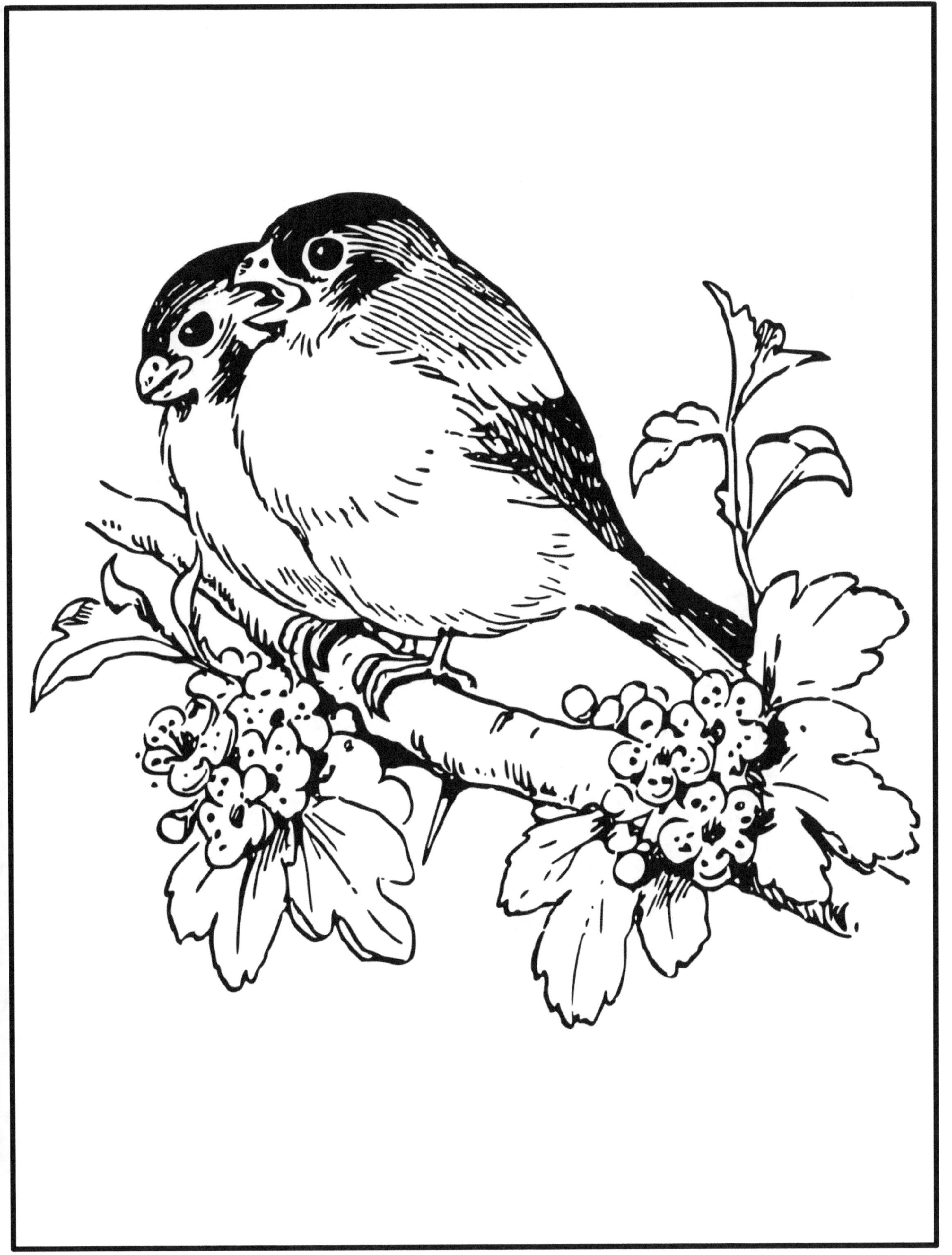

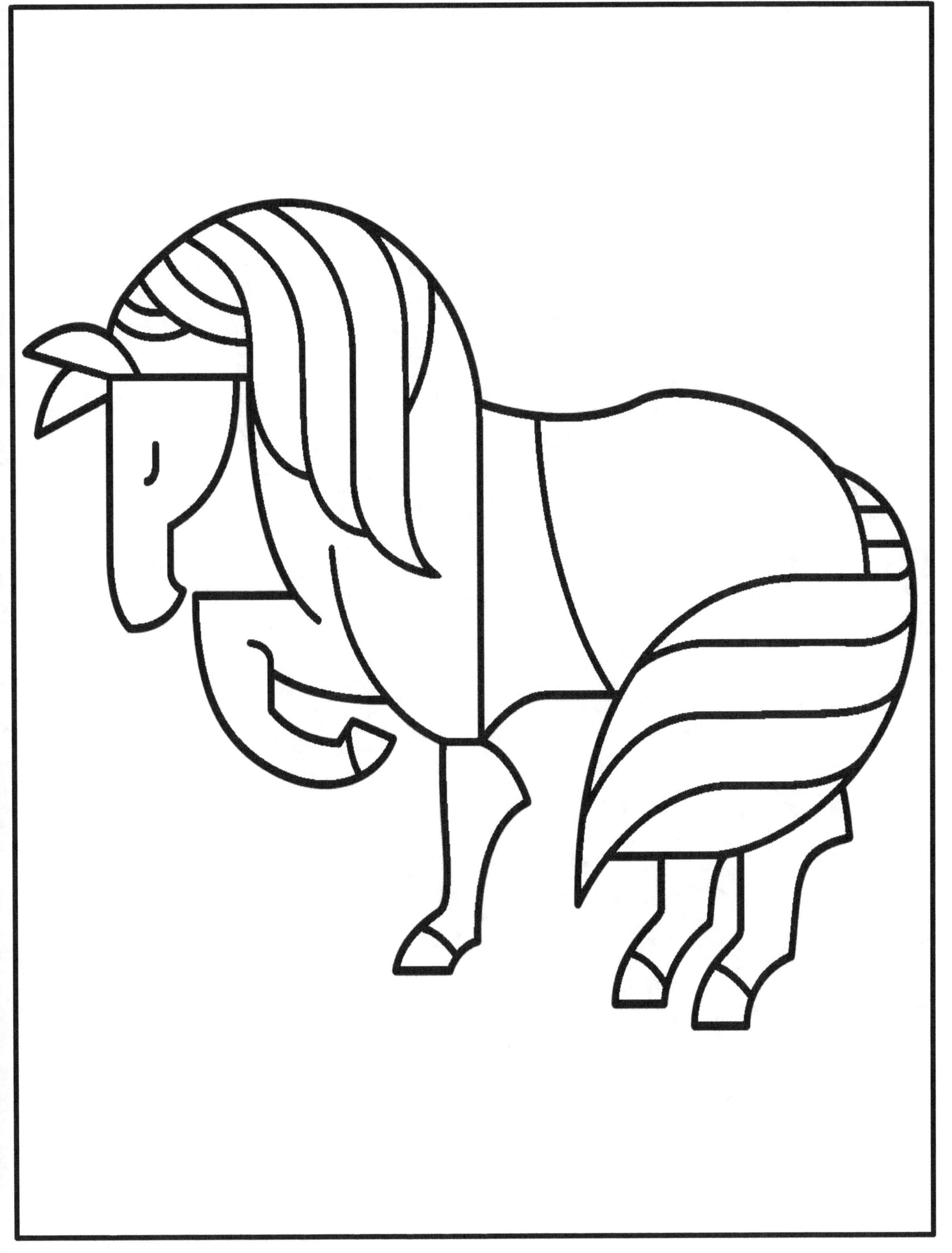

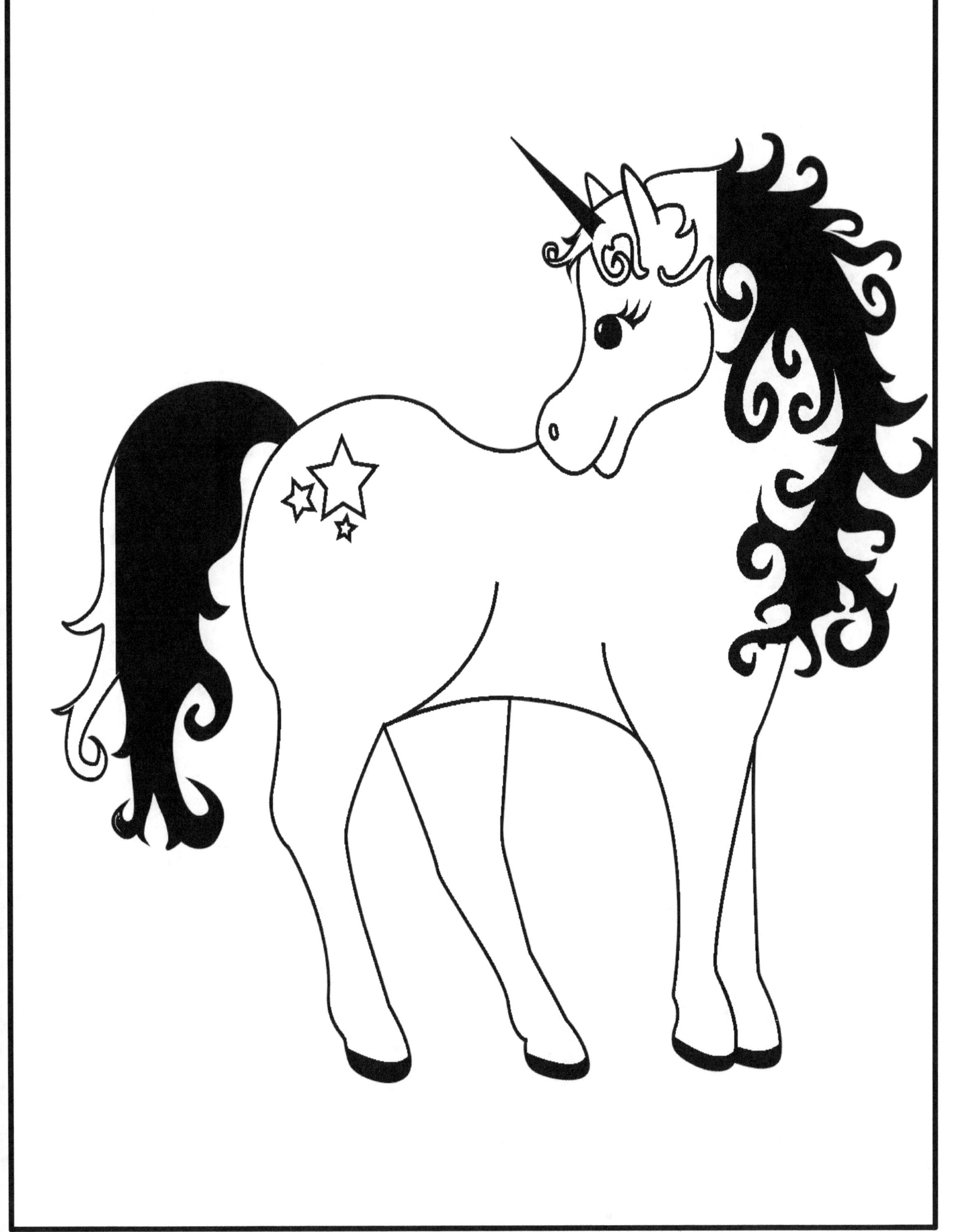

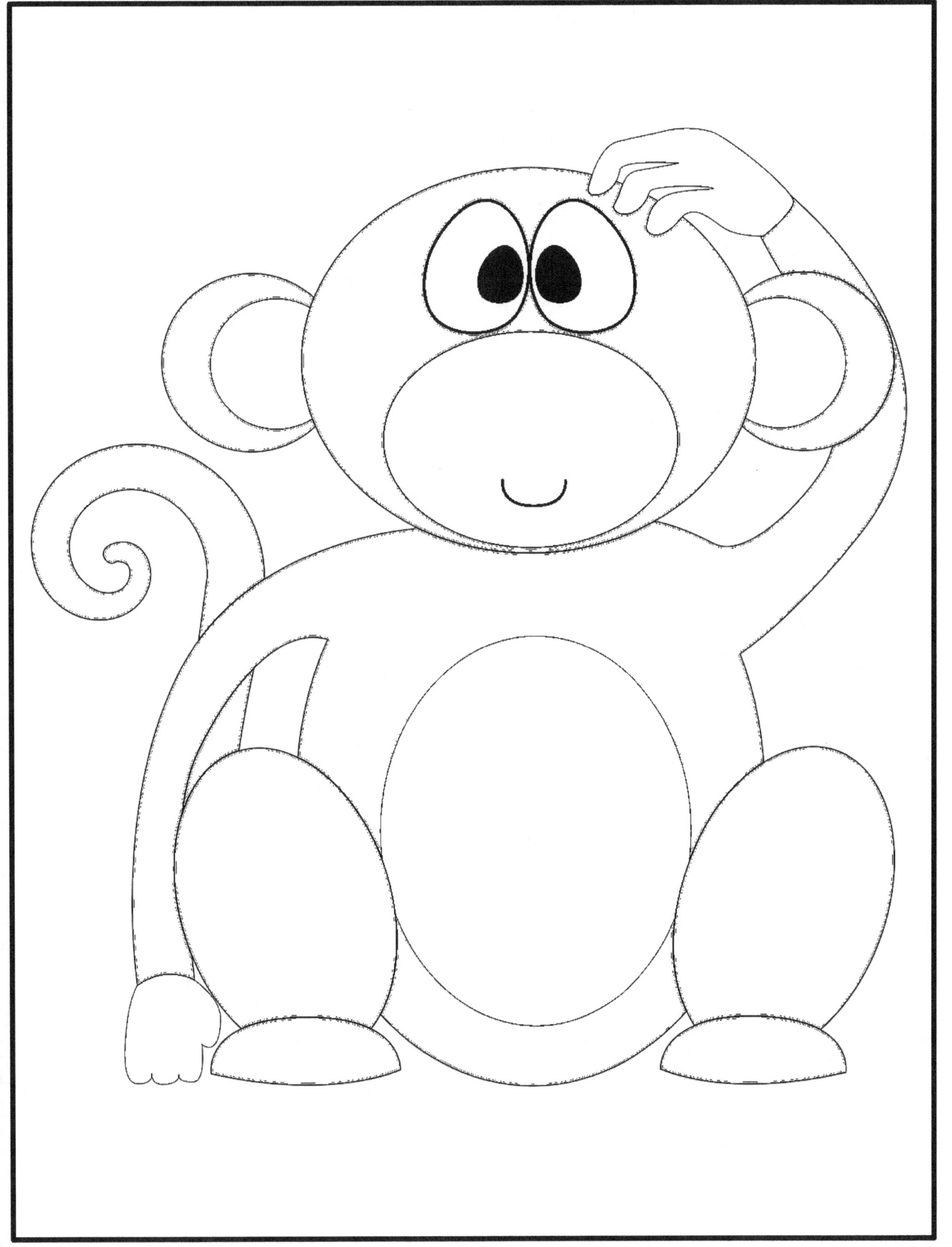

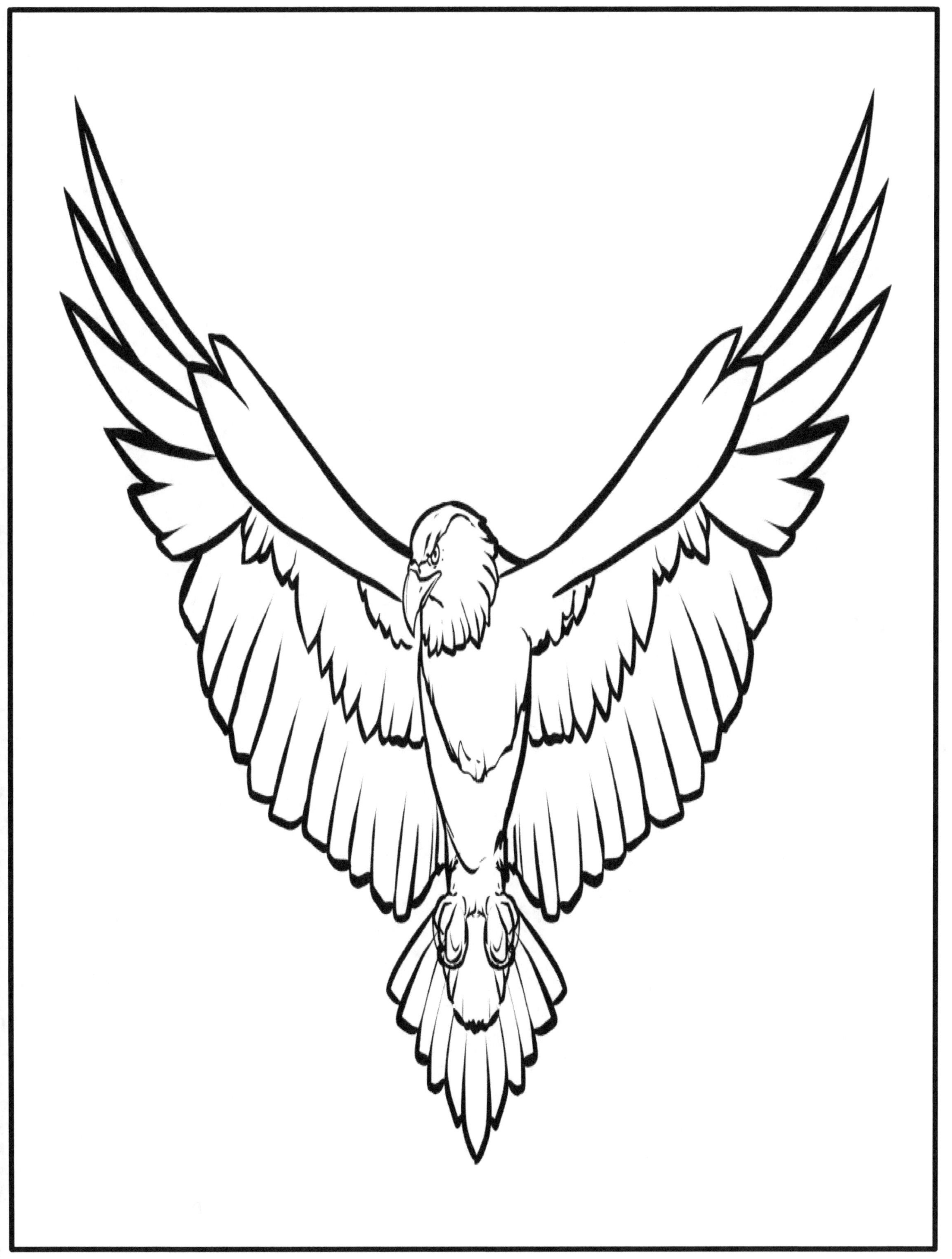

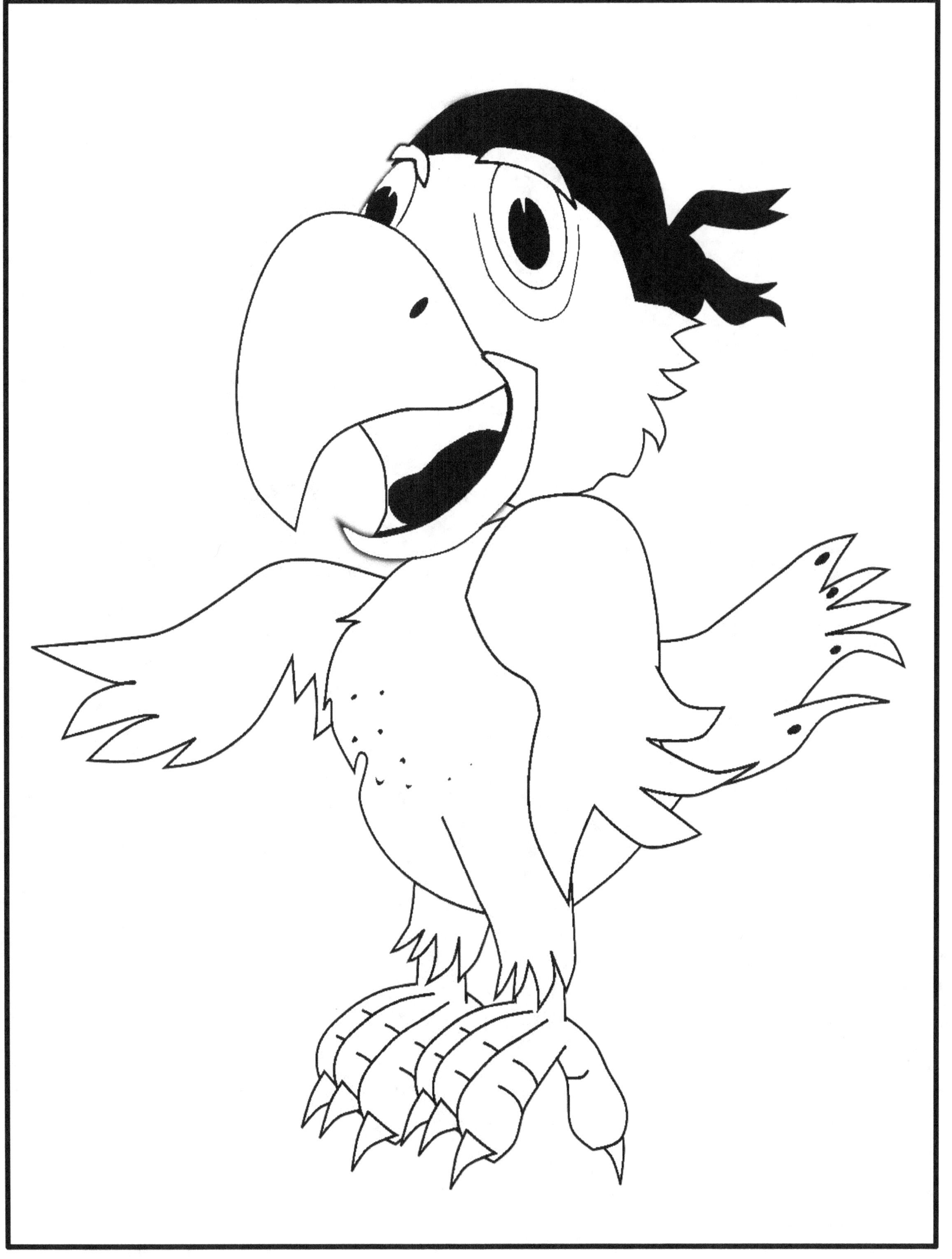

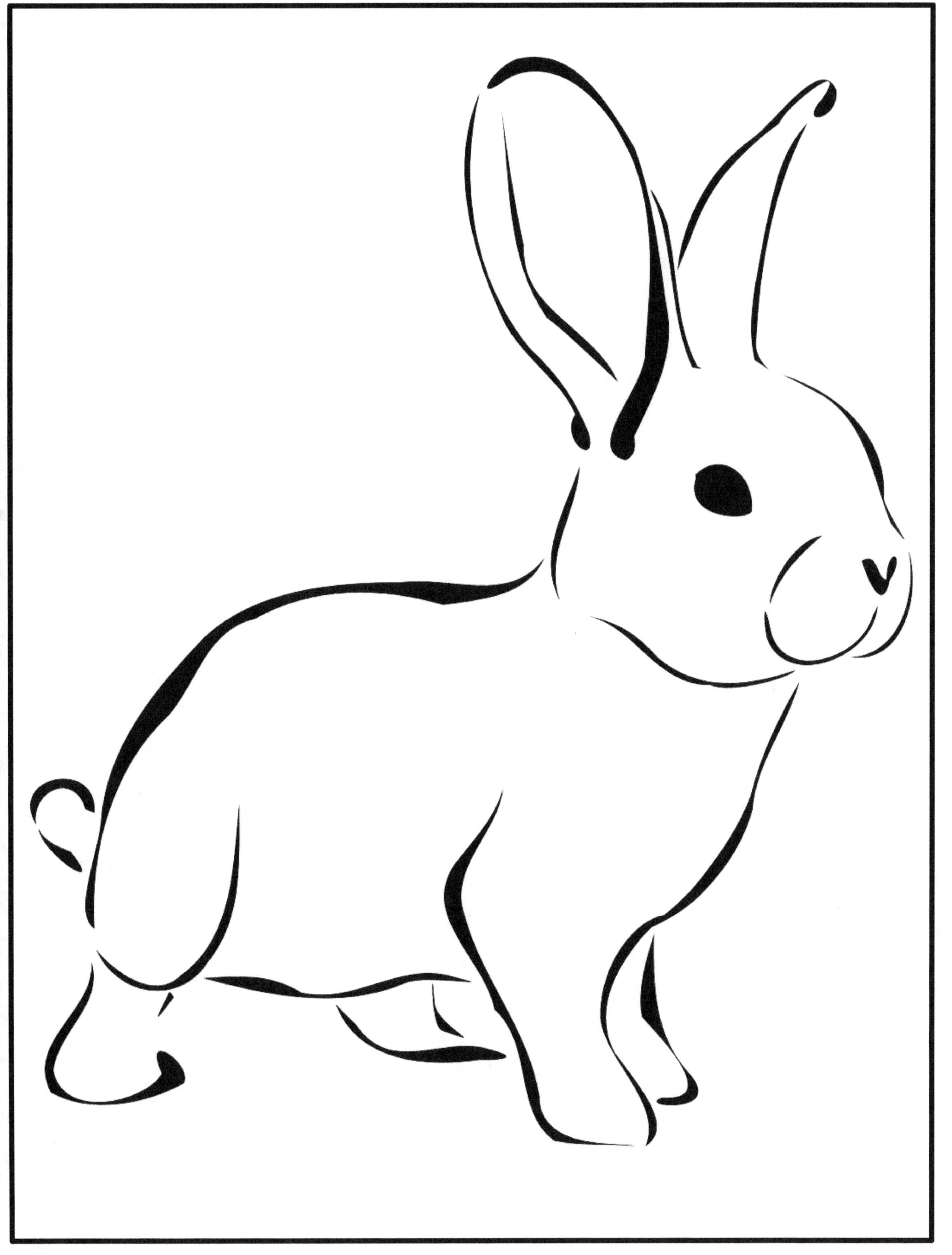